Library of
Davidson College

HARVARD HISTORICAL MONOGRAPHS
XIX

PUBLISHED UNDER THE DIRECTION OF THE DEPARTMENT
OF HISTORY FROM THE INCOME OF

THE ROBERT LOUIS STROOCK FUND

Vassi and Fideles in the Carolingian Empire

BY

CHARLES EDWIN ODEGAARD

OCTAGON BOOKS

A DIVISION OF FARRAR, STRAUS AND GIROUX

New York   1972

Copyright, 1945 by the President and Fellows of Harvard College

Reprinted 1972
by special arrangement with Harvard University Press

OCTAGON BOOKS
A DIVISION OF FARRAR, STRAUS & GIROUX, INC.
19 Union Square West
New York, N. Y. 10003

LIBRARY OF CONGRESS CATALOG CARD NUMBER: 70-159217

ISBN 0-374-96135-2

Printed in U.S.A. by
NOBLE OFFSET PRINTERS, INC.
NEW YORK 3, N. Y.

To
My Mother and Father

True views on Mediaevalism Time alone will bring
But, as far as we can judge, it's something like this sort of thing:
    You hold yourself like this
    You hold yourself like that
By hook and crook you try to look both angular and flat

— Patience

PREFACE

THE SUBJECT of this study may at first glance strike the reader as remarkably confined, for the historian interested in the political institutions of the earlier Middle Ages is accustomed to treatises which travel in seven-league boots such as those of Waitz, Brunner, and Fustel de Coulanges. Accordingly, the reader might suppose that the material presented here would be a heavy load of minutiae the general sense of which could be found already in the more expansive works. The genesis of this study, however, belies any such assumption, for its roots lie far afield. It was certainly not the end in view when I began research upon the political status of the French bishops in the twelfth and thirteenth centuries. It is none the less a product of investigations begun in this later field, for I found certain difficulties in the existing treatises which prevented an immediate solution of my original problem until the "background" was cleared. That in itself has proved to be no easy task.

The "static quality" of the Middle Ages is a concept which no medievalist is now likely to accept, yet not infrequently there has been written sober medieval history which assumes, perhaps unconsciously, relatively unchanging conditions. Such an assumption surely underlies much lumping together of texts from widely different times and places and the application of the same terms and ideas to very different settings. It is important not to overlook the possible changes in terms within fairly restricted periods, changes such as those forcefully attested by a monk of Saint Père de Chartres named Paul who, living in the eleventh century, "speaks of a collection of charters, the most ancient of which dated from the ninth century: 'What changes! The rolls preserved in the archives of our abbey show that the peasants of that time lived under customs which those of today know no longer; even the words which they used are not those of the present day.' And further on: 'I have found the names of places, persons, and things changed since that time to such a degree that not only have they disappeared, but it is no longer possible to identify them; far from having preserved them, men do not even know them.' " [1]

In an effort to avoid such a misuse of the sources the following study of certain aspects of vassalage will be confined to a relatively restricted period, that extending from 751 to 888. The choice of this period is not dependent upon caprice. This period with its capitularies and annals is the first to provide historians with adequate material for the study of the *vassi*. Furthermore, this period has a certain intrinsic unity which permits the materials from it reasonably to be grouped together for a study of its political institutions. It is both preceded and followed by a period of weakness on the part of the monarchy and by the disorganization of political life. But within this period the monarchy was strong enough to make itself a unifying force, to maintain an administration running throughout the Frankish realm, and to make itself felt at least in a measure by all men. In the last years of the ninth century the Frankish monarchy was foundering; the consolidation of royal power had given way to the dissolution of royal power. All governmental institutions, and vassalage among them, were affected by this cardinal fact. It seems especially desirable then for us to make a study of the nature of vassalage within this period, a study which is quite possible because of the manifold sources which have survived. Furthermore, it is imperative that this Carolingian material be considered on its own merits as the best evidence for Carolingian conditions and that sources from later times be conscientiously rejected for the purposes of this study.[2] Whatever vassalage may have become in later times under very different circumstances, we shall by following this procedure have a better understanding of Carolingian vassalage.

C. E. O.

CONTENTS

I	INTRODUCTION	3
II	VASSI	14
III	FIDELES	51
IV	CONCLUSION	69

APPENDICES

I	Commendation and the Oath of Fidelity	75
II	Further Difficulties Concerning Vassalage	80
III	The Bishop's Letter from Kiersy in 858	85
IV	Krawinkel's Interpretation of the Tassilo Case	90
V	Fustel de Coulanges on Fideles	97
VI	Bibliography	98
	Notes	110
	Abbreviations	158
	Index	159

CHAPTER I

INTRODUCTION

THE practical circumstances of life in the Frankish empire occasion a division of the free men into two main groups.[1] The first of these consists of the rank and file, the ordinary "subjects" as they are usually called. Certainly most of these men rarely if ever saw the king; when they did see him, it was probably only a glimpse of him as he slowly perambulated through the kingdom. These men could in the nature of things rarely be of any immediate use to the king. Obedient to the king's commands they should be; truly useful for the king's military purposes in any but a very limited way they could not be. The frontiers of the Frankish state under the Carolingians were far flung. The man who could travel far had perforce to be a man of means. Men of modest income could doubtless go to a war which was being fought close to their homes, but the expanding boundaries of the Frankish empire must have left many subjects of the king far from the fighting area. The ordinary subject, whatever his obligations in law, must have lacked the means of fighting for a king who did not pay his men a salary, who did not provide them with arms or supplies, and who forbade their pillaging within the boundaries of the kingdom. The almost constant wars of the Carolingian period would most certainly have entailed the disappearance of agriculture and brought famine in their train if the bulk of the population had done the fighting. The seasoned regular fighters had of necessity to be men with the means needed to maintain them and their retinue far from home; they had to be landowners with resources large enough to support retainers and servants who could manage their estates while they were away. They had to be, in other words, not ordinary subjects but rather men of substance, *primores, primates, magnates, magni,* or *majores* of the realm.

Waging war was not the only function of the king. He had also the business of running his kingdom: managing his own estates, conducting diplomacy, preserving the peace, maintaining the courts of justice, supervising the rudimentary public works of the time, and collecting the money and goods necessary for the maintenance of himself and his associates. For all these tasks he had to have an administrative personnel.

It was beyond the realm of possibility for the Carolingian king to support this staff by paying salaries. He was forced, instead, to rely on services exacted from those of his subjects who were rich enough to devote their time to serving him or from favored friends whom he endowed with benefices. It mattered little whether the wealth of these servants came from lands possessed by them in their own right or through the loan or gift of the king, or from the occupation of an endowed office such as a bishopric or abbey. Regardless of the title by which they held their lands, they were in a position to be able to serve the king. Between these richer subjects upon whom the king relied for service of all kinds and the king there was certain to be a relationship differing from the bond between the ordinary subjects and the king. There is general agreement among historians to the effect that the special status characteristic of the royal servants was acquired by the performance of a secular act known as commendation to

INTRODUCTION 5

which there may be joined a religious guarantee, the oath of fidelity.[2] Commendation was entered not merely by royal servants but also by men who served other lords. Men commended themselves for service (*commendaverunt se in manus Hittonis episcopi ad servitium*).[3] To indicate the act of commendation the texts use besides *se commendare* its synonyms, *se committere, se tradere, se dedere, se accommodare, se praebere*,[4] often together with *manibus junctis, manibus*, or *in manus*.[5] The man who commends himself places himself in the hands of a seignior.[6] The latter is sometimes designated in the texts as *dominus*[7] but more frequently as *senior*.[8] The rôle of the seignior in an act of commendation is described as "receiving" (*suscipere*) the man who is making the commendation.[9]

The king accordingly has a dual status; he is a king ruling over subjects and at the same time a seignior who receives the actual service of certain individuals who commend themselves to him. The purpose of this study is to determine the general terms used in Carolingian times for these royal servants. There is a marked tendency to refer to them as vassals. As Fustel de Coulanges says, the king has two kinds of subjects; for some, as their king and emperor, he is the head of the State; for others, as their seignior and patron, he is the leader of *"vassals."*[10] According to Pfister the client who entered commendation "was called *vassus*."[11] This same use of the term "vassal" for any man who had commended himself occurs many times in historical literature.[12]

The highest functionaries of the realm were royal servants, and it is a common practice to speak of them as "vassals." For example, Declareuil says that all the magnates and consequently the king's functionaries were his "vassals."[13] Pfister elaborates upon this by saying that the king considered as his "vassals" conquered or dependent princes, princes of the royal family, dukes, counts, bishops, and abbots.[14] At the hands of Pirenne the very basis of the king's government becomes "vassalage," for he says that "in the ninth century the kings exacted an oath of vassalage from all the magnates of the kingdom, and even from the bishops. It became increasingly apparent that only those were truly submissive to the king who had paid homage to him. Thus the subject was disappearing behind the vassal."[15] Furthermore, "Charlemagne's Empire was based on vassalage. Charles had hoped to govern by means of his vassals and urged men to become vassals of these vassals."[16] Numerous instances may be cited showing this practice of calling the king's magnates and functionaries, lay and ecclesiastical, "vassals."[17]

When one reads carefully, however, the statements of a number of historians who have devoted by and large the greatest attention to the subject of vassalage, one detects disharmonious notes, reservations, hesitations. Let us look at a few cases in detail.

Some of Waitz's remarks appear consistent with the opinion already presented. He says bluntly enough that one who has commended himself is known as a "vassal"; the latter word is used in the most varied connections, for lesser landowners who have received their hide of land from a religious foundation or some other lord, for abbots, for magnates, and for foreign princes who for special reasons have entered this relationship, that is, *vassaticum*.[18] He asserts, likewise, that foreign princes who subjected themselves to Pepin I and his successors swore the vassals' oath; one of these, he notes, is actually called a vassal.[19]

INTRODUCTION

His texts justifying this assertion show how closely he identifies commendation with vassalage; with the exception of the text [20] to which he specifically calls attention the others all refer to acts of commendation with no mention of the word "vassal" or "vassalage."[21] Waitz even calls a deacon a "vassal" though the text says only that he had given himself *in militiae servitutem*, that is, had commended himself into service.[22]

So far Waitz has stated the case clearly for the identity of commendation with vassalage regardless of the status of the person commending himself. This certainty is lacking in other passages where one finds strained circumlocutions. He says, for example, that the higher functionaries felt the influence of vassalage and so they were clearly regarded and designated as vassals. (Is there a reservation here? *Are* they vassals, or are they only regarded and designated as vassals in some limited sense?) Waitz continues, saying that the abbots entered a commendation which does not differ from commendation into vassalage. (Are abbots then really vassals?) Even the bishops recognize themselves to be the king's vassals. He adds, however, that the bishops in the ninth century struggled against the *real* (*eigentlich*) vassal's oath of allegiance. The oath which the bishops swore varied from that of the lay magnates. It reflected their spiritual office, but contained at least the promise to be faithful as a vassal should be to his lord.[23] Elsewhere, he says that there were clergy who entered royal service, bishops who commended themselves to the king, though this relationship is not clearly to be interpreted as vassalage. Where vassalage is to be established, the oath of fidelity must be given; it is the determining element in vassalage.[24] But as we have just seen, the bishops in the ninth century swore an oath which differed from that of the laity. Are they then, we may ask, really vassals? In what sense are they vassals?

These doubts and ambiguities appear again. Waitz says that vassalage influenced the relation between the counts and the king and between the lesser officials and the counts, so that frequently vassals were given these official positions; in many respects vassals and officials are regarded as the same.[25] Waitz does not distinguish these relationships very clearly; he seems to have felt that officials were somehow not vassals. He says also that members of the royal family, like the officials and magnates, now commend themselves to the king and swear oaths which actually fall into the category which the *real* vassals (*eigentliche Vassallen*) swear when they perform commendation.[26] Real vassals! What kind of vassals then are these royal princes, bishops, abbots, counts, and lesser officials?

Similar difficulties arise in an attempt to interpret the meaning of Guilhiermoz. He begins in an orthodox manner by saying that the Carolingians saw in vassalage a means of attaching to themselves by narrow and humiliating bonds all those who might be dangerous to them; so they imposed it upon foreign princes seeking their aid, and upon the magnates of the kingdom including the members of the royal family and even their sons.[27] But these men are, it seems, not quite vassals. For them, he says, vassalage is only accessory, *le caractère vassalique* is added to something else.[28] These men are not to be confused with the royal vassals properly so called, that is, men for whom this title, far from being a disgrace, is an honor attended by considerable advantages.[29] The counts and great magnates are not *really* vassals, are not vassals *proprement dits*; they have *le caractère vassalique*, be-

INTRODUCTION 9

cause they have made *l'hommage vassalique* to the king; because, it would seem, commendation makes a man a vassal, if not a real vassal!

Mitteis, conscious of the presence of difficulties, does not gloss them over although he offers no clear solution to the problem. He describes a vassal as one who has commended himself to the service of a lord or seignior and says that from the beginning vassalage has gone with the ceremony of commendation by which the hands of the vassal are put into the hands of the seignior.[30] Carolingian princes,[31] foreign princes,[32] and bishops [33] become vassals by commendation. Elsewhere he refers to the idea that all the officials were the king's vassals, only to reject it halfheartedly, saying that it cannot be asserted with full assurance.[34] His reasoning seems to be this. 1) As we have noted, he regards men who have commended themselves as vassals, as men who have pledged themselves to the *vassallitischen Huldigung*. 2) As a consequence of this they must undertake the responsibilities of official functions.[35] 3) But the officials, that is, bishops, abbots, dukes, counts, and lesser functionaries seem to be distinguished from vassals in many texts. 4) These officials have entered a *Beamtendienst* (by what procedure it is not said), which carries with it presumably the responsibilities of official duties, but not the necessity of performing [*vassallitischen*] *Huldigung*. 5) Hence vassals and officials are not really the same.

Even when no difficulties are seen with regard to the "vassalage" of counts, perplexities sometimes arise insofar as the bishops are concerned. Fustel de Coulanges betrays no hesitancy in regarding counts as vassals. He says that counts are above all royal functionaries; but they have another character at the same time, that is, vassalage.

Counts always began their careers in the palace service which they entered by commending themselves to become the king's faithful servants (*fidèles*). They did not renounce this fidelity the day the king gave them a county; they regarded themselves as the vassals and beneficiaries of the king rather than as representatives of the public authority. "All these ideas, however, are so confused that in the language of the time a county was regarded as a benefice." And the count was a vassal.[36] With regard to the bishops, however, Fustel de Coulanges is less definite in his assertions. The bishop commends himself and his church to the king in an act of homage which is *approximately* (*à peu de chose près*) the same as that of lay beneficiaries. The contract is conceived in the same terms and produces *almost* (*à peu près*) the same effects.[37] *À peu de chose près, à peu près!* Why these reservations? If they are not the same, in what way do they differ? No answer is forthcoming. These reservations are not effective enough to keep him from calling the bishop a vassal in the very next sentence.[38]

Imbart de la Tour recognizes the existence of a distinction between bishops and vassals but he fails to detect the basis for the distinction. He says that bishops, abbots, counts, and vassals are distinguished one from another, but in any case the distinction between the obligations of the bishop and those of the vassal is so small that none appears in the texts and none can be discovered from a minute analysis of the documents.[39] He must have realized that this statement was somewhat unsatisfying, for he adds that one would not be surprised at this state of affairs if he recalled that the bishop, like the count, is a functionary and that at the end of the ninth century every honor granted by the king places upon the recipient a

INTRODUCTION

special dependent status which is ordinarily indicated by vassalage.[40] This "explanation" seems only to reassert that the bishops are vassals, without indicating how bishops are distinguished from vassals.

It is evident from this brief survey [41] that difficulty has been encountered in allocating the place of vassals in the service relationship, in determining the position of vassals among dependents in general who render service in return for protection. There are two main tendencies. On the one hand, some historians describe all those who have commended themselves to the seignior as "vassals"; the *vassus* and the *commendatus* are one and the same thing. Vassalage is the bond or contract established when a man commends himself to the service and protection of the king, and it regularly includes, besides men who are specifically called vassals, bishops, abbots, counts and other functionaries, and great magnates. With vassalage thus conceived, the vassals form a broad group of dependents who render service.

On the other hand, most historians recognize that there is some difference between men who are considered as, or treated as, vassals, such as bishops, abbots, counts, functionaries, and great magnates, on the one hand; and on the other "real" vassals or *vassaux proprement dits*. The former are only *à peu près* vassals or have only *le caractère vassalique*: some of them act like vassals, yet they are not actually called vassals. The bishops in particular are somehow different from the vassals although that difference is apparently not demonstrable. With vassalage thus conceived, "real" vassals form a narrow class within the broad group of dependents who render service. Yet the basis of the distinction between "real" vassals and vassals in general is not made clear; there is some doubt even whether the bishops, abbots, counts, and great magnates are really vassals at all.

It is not by any means a *reductio ad absurdum* to ask this question: if men who are vassals are not really vassals, then what are vassals? Or, to state the problem in a better way, what are the criteria by which one may distinguish vassals from other men? The first question then leads to a second question: if the king's servants in general are not to be called "vassals," then what general term should be used to cover this category?

This is really a problem in terminology, in deciding what is meant by "vassal." The terminology of historians who have dealt with this subject has become hopelessly confused with the result that there is a crying need for its standardization. The only basis for such a standardization should be to the greatest extent possible the language of the texts themselves. Each change in word or expression may carry with it new overtones, new connotations which may lead to misunderstanding. Indeed, we modern historians should cling as closely as possible to the words of the Carolingians; for every gap between their words and ours, there may occur unsuspected a further gap between their concept and ours. To be certain of recapturing the thought of men long dead, we must not only employ that historical imagination by which we guess at their concepts; we must also check our hypotheses at every step against what they have actually said, word for word, for their words are closer to their thoughts than ours can ever be. Indeed, now that they themselves are dead, their own words are the tests which in the last analysis our reconstructions of their thoughts must pass.

The method used here, then, will be to present an hypothesis which conforms as closely as possible to the actual language of the contemporary texts. Insofar as it is possible, the texts shall speak for themselves in their own words. Thus a careful scrutiny of the pattern of these words may reveal the thought pattern which dictated their original choice and may disprove any of the thought patterns which may wrongly have been attributed to them.

CHAPTER II

VASSI

I

WE SHALL now proceed to investigate the use of the term *vassi* or *vassalli* in Carolingian sources.

The term occurs frequently in texts where it denotes a category of men distinct from the higher officials such as bishops, abbots, and counts. An example may be found in a capitulary [42] ascribed to Louis the Pious which mentions disputes over tithes between a bishop or other priests on the one hand, and on the other hand, counts, vassals, and other *fideles*.[43] The writer of the capitulary must have thought of the vassals as different from the counts or from bishops and other priests. We find the same distinctions made elsewhere. The *Annales Bertiniani* gives the list of those who commended themselves to Charles the Bald in 837 as bishops, abbots, counts, *and royal vassals* [44] (*vassalli dominici*) and of those who commended themselves to Louis II of France in 877 as bishops, abbots, *primores* of the realm, and *royal vassals* (*vassalli regii*).[45] In a capitulary concerning taxation, a matter in which one would expect a precise indication of the categories of persons assessed, we find bishops, abbots, counts, *and royal vassals* named in that order.[46] One chapter of the *Capitularia De Disciplina Palatii Aquisgranensis* concerns itself with the residence at Aachen of bishops, abbots, counts, *and vassals*.[47] According to the *Vita Hludowici Imperatoris* there were present at the funeral of Louis the Pious, Drogo, bishop of Metz, and other bishops, abbots, counts, *royal vassals*, and a great crowd of clergy and laity.[48] Charles the Bald and Louis the German met for a *colloquium* at Meersen in 870; with good reason neither trusted the other, and so it was arranged in advance that each would appear at the meeting with an equal number of men chosen from predetermined groups: [49] namely, four bishops, ten counsellors, and thirty men from among the functionaries (*ministeriales*)[50] *and vassals.* When Charles the Fat sat in judgment at Siena in 881, he had the assistance of one marquis, eight counts, six *vassals*, two judges, one papal count and many other men.[51] The existence of a plenitude[52] of such texts as these in which vassals are found specifically mentioned after bishops, abbots, and counts must lead one to doubt that this is mere redundancy on the part of the various authors of these texts,[53] that bishops, abbots, and counts are merely types of vassals as so many historians have thought, and cause one to suspect that vassals are men different from bishops, abbots, and counts, that they are in fact a separate group.

This suspicion must become a conviction in the face of the following texts. Charlemagne established in Aquitaine counts, abbots, and many *other men who are commonly called vassals*. It is not the counts and abbots but rather *other men* who are called vassals.[54] When bishops, abbots, and counts act as *missi*, under certain conditions they are not to receive the gifts (*coniectum*) of their "constituents"; but no such limitation is put upon lesser functionaries (*ministeriales*) and vassals when they act as *missi*.[55] If bishops, abbots, and counts were at the same time vassals, this capitulary would be senseless; therefore, bishops, abbots, and counts must not be vassals. In fact vassals are not only different from bishops, abbots, counts, and *ministeriales*; they are definitely inferior in rank (*qualitas*) to these, and so when they act as *missi*, they may require fewer supplies from the people than may abbots, counts, and *ministeriales*, and these in turn may require less than a bishop.[56]

Other evidence supports the view that vassals are men who have an inferior rank among royal servants. They do not seem to be included among the *primores* of the realm, for a capitulary of 877 names the vassals after the *primores* in a list of those who commended themselves to Louis II.[57] Had the vassals been included among the *primores*, Hincmar would probably not have mentioned them. One might infer also that vassals are of lower rank than bishops, abbots, and counts from the fact that they are named only *after* bishops, abbots, and counts.[58]

It is not surprising that the term "vassal" is used for a servant who is not of the very highest rank, for *vassus* was originally applied to an unfree servant.[59] But in the eighth century we find free men designated as vassals,[60] the oldest certain case being in the *Lex Alamanni*, dating from between 709 and 739.[61] Thenceforth *vassus* mounted in the social scale, but it occasionally was used in the ninth century and even later of unfree servants.[62] Throughout the middle ages, in fact, traces of the servile origin of vassalage remained at least in terminology.[63]

The conclusion to which one must come on the basis of texts so far presented is that vassals fall into a category quite separate from those of bishops, abbots, and counts and that they are of a rank inferior to that of these great officials. We can detect certain other characteristics in which vassals seem to differ from these officials. In the Carolingian period the count is a functionary who represents the royal authority in a definite area, who rules in a sense as viceroy in his county (*comitatus*).[64] He is a royal functionary and serves only the king; only the latter has counts under his command. Similarly the bishop is in charge of a bishopric, a geographical circumscription (*parochia*) within the kingdom, and he serves not only God, but also the king. No private persons have bishops in their service. Vassals, however, are not functionaries of this kind. They have no definite territory assigned to them as an administrative portion of the kingdom; there is no territorial *vassaticum* to correspond to the *comitatus* or *parochia*. Furthermore, whereas bishops and counts do not serve private persons, vassals do serve men other than the king, for besides the royal vassals, there are the vassals of bishops, abbots, abbesses, and counts,[65] and even of royal vassals.[66] A vassal who was in the service of one man could apparently, with the permission of his seignior, transfer himself to the service of a new seignior.[67] One cannot imagine a situation in which the king would permit his bishops and counts to transfer their service to another seignior, although, as we have seen, it is possible for a man who is called a vassal to transfer his service to another. It was probably the vassals among others, then, whom Charles the Bald had in mind when he made certain concessions to ward off a revolt in 856; he gave his consent to those who were dissatisfied with serving him to transfer themselves to the service of another seignior.[68] He could hardly have permitted bishops and counts to abandon him.

Vassals might of course be used as *missi*, men sent to conduct specific business for the king such as the handling of fiscal matters.[69] But the position of a *missus* was not a regular function; men of various ranks, bishops, abbots, counts, and *ministeriales* as well as vassals, might be called upon by the king to act as *missi* for him.⁷⁰ It was not because they occasionally acted as *missi* that vassals were distinguished from other men, but rather because they had a certain function⁷¹ which they regularly performed for their seignior. That function was sufficiently specialized to result in the establishment of a definite category for those who performed it. A vassal is, as we shall now see, a man who commends himself to his seignior to serve above all as a properly equipped and properly trained armed retainer.⁷²

An illuminating text is contained in a letter written by Hincmar of Rheims to his recalcitrant nephew, Hincmar, bishop of Laon. The uncle urged the young man to reform and to abandon his evil ways. Among other things the uncle wrote, "Many say that you show pride in the strength (*fortitudine*) and agility of your body, and that you converse frequently and freely about fighting (*de proeliis*) and, as we say in our language, *de vassaticis*, and that you talk irreverently about how you would act if you were a layman and about other things which are neither proper for you to say or to do, nor for me to mention."⁷³ In this interesting passage, *vassaticum* is placed between exercising the strength of the body and fighting on the one hand, and on the other, doing what laymen do and what clerics should not do. Hincmar must have been thinking of the numerous canonical proscriptions against the bearing of arms by clerics.⁷⁴ Vassalage must have something to do with fighting and the bearing of arms.

There is ample evidence in other texts to bear out this conjecture. Vassals are men before whose wisdom and strength (*fortitudo*)⁷⁵ it is not safe to show any hot temper or resistance.⁷⁶ Vassals are armed men. Only to their vassals are bishops and abbots to give arms.⁷⁷ Slaves who are honored by their lords with vassalage receive horses and arms,[78] and must swear the general oath of fidelity to the king. There is no need to interpret the function of these unfree vassals as in any sense different from that of free vassals. A slave given a horse and arms and properly trained could make just as effective a soldier as a free man and could be just as dangerous to the king. Consequently, unfree men who had been honored by their masters with vassalage had to swear to be loyal subjects of the king.

We find men called *vassals* performing tasks for which armed retainers would be well fitted. Counts and lesser judges can, if need be, call upon the vassals of bishops to help them in pursuing and capturing bandits.[79] Furthermore, *vassals* are established on the frontiers to guard them,[80] and are sent, along with counts and abbots, into regions restless under Carolingian rule such as Aquitaine in the days of Charlemagne.[81] In those regions counts, abbots, and vassals had to care for the administration of the realm, the protection of the frontiers, and the supervision of the royal *villae*. Counts and abbots would be few in numbers and the burden of guarding the frontiers would presumably call for a larger proportion of vassals. When Charlemagne wrote Fastrade about an encounter between Pepin and the Avars, he indicated that the Frankish participants were one bishop, two dukes including the duke of Istria with his men, two counts and an undisclosed number of royal vassals.[82] The exact number of vassals was probably omitted because it would be larger and accordingly more difficult to determine.

It is the business of men called vassals, whether the king's or other men's, to appear in the army, and in the case of vassals who are in the service of private men, it is up to the seigniors to see that they put in an appearance in the king's army or bear the consequences. Louis II of Italy ordered before his Beneventan expedition of 866 that counts and royal vassals who failed to appear in the army and that abbots and abbesses who failed to send their men should lose their *honores*, while their vassals should be deprived of their own property and their benefices. Bishops who were similarly remiss should lose their benefices as well as their own property.[83] Louis the Pious ordered in 819 that vassals who failed to appear in the army that year, whether they were his own vassals or those of bishops, abbots, abbesses, and counts, should pay a fine unless they had a good excuse.[84] His list of possible excuses shows what sorts of things vassals might legitimately be doing if they were not serving in the army. They might remain away from the army to exercise their brawn in maintaining the peace for the count [85] or guarding the latter's wife and home; or in maintaining the peace for bishops, abbots, and abbesses (probably on their immunities) or in disciplining the dependents of these (*familiam constringendam*), or in gathering their revenues[86] and caring for *missi*.

The inferior rank of vassals as well as their preoccupation with fighting (*proeliis*) is indicated in a curious passage written by Walafrid Strabo.[87] He compares secular government with ecclesiastical, the royal administration with the administration of the church. Each is a hierarchy with a series of parallel officers. He says that just as the Roman emperors are said to have been the monarchs of the whole world, so the pontiff of the see of Rome, filling the place of the Apostle Peter, is at the very head of all the church. We may compare archbishops to kings, metropolitans to dukes. What the counts and prefects perform

VASSI 21

in the secular world, the bishops do in the church. "Just as there are praetors or *comites palatii* who hear the cases of secular men, so there are the men whom the Franks call the highest chaplains who preside over the cases of clerics. The lesser chaplains are just like those whom we call in Gallic fashion the lord's vassals (*vassos dominicos*). The chaplains (*cappellani*) were first so named from the cape (*cappa*) of St. Martin which the kings of the Franks were accustomed to carry with them to help them secure the victory in battle (*ob adiutorium victoriae in proeliis*); they were called chaplains because they were the clerics who cared for and guarded (*ferentes et custodientes*) the cape along with other relics of the saints." The king's vassals then may be compared to relatively inferior members of the ecclesiastical hierarchy, the lesser chaplains who guard the relic which assures victory in battle. The military character of vassals and their inferior position in the hierarchy of functionaries could not be better illustrated.

The monk of St. Gall in his life of Charlemagne described the order in which men at the *palatium* of the emperor dined.[88] First came Charlemagne himself with dukes and rulers (*tiranni*) and kings of various people. "After them it was the turn of counts and prefects, and chiefs of the various branches of the government (*diversarum dignitatum proceres*). When they had finished eating, the military men or palace bodyguard (*militares viri vel scolares auli*) were given food. After them the men in charge of all the offices were fed, and then the servants (*ministri*) and then the lowest servants (*ministrorum ministri*), so that it was the middle of the night before all had eaten." This passage parallels in part the indications of rank given by Louis the Pious in his capitulary of 819 concerning the *coniectum* to be given to *missi*.[89] There the vassals are indicated as being of lower rank than bishops, abbots, counts, and *ministeriales*. In the monk's account, the *militares viri vel scolares auli* are of lower rank than the counts and prefects and *diversarum dignitatum proceres*; the military men, presumably vassals, are inferior in rank to the great officers of state, counts and bishops.

Vassals then may act as *missi* as do other functionaries who serve their seignior, but when one thinks of vassals, one thinks of fighters.[90] Vassals are the armed men who are used for guarding the frontiers, for putting down resistance, and for police, and who are especially obliged to give military service.

The need for specialized service of this kind is easy to understand from a review of conditions in the Carolingian period. It is true that under the Carolingians all men in the realm may be called upon to fight for the king,[91] whether possessors of property or not.[92] In the case of an invasion of the realm, all without exception, free or unfree, might be called upon to aid in the protection of the land.[93] But the king did not provide for the maintenance of his soldiers while campaigning; they were paid no salary.[94] They were permitted to collect water, firewood, fodder, and straw from the countryside through which they passed[95] but that was all; measures were taken to see that the army moved through the kingdom in good order without inflicting injuries on anyone.[96] The soldiers were expected to provide for their own maintenance, at times with supplies of food for three months of marching, and of clothing for six months;[97] and they were expected to procure their own arms.[98] Under Charlemagne and his successors long campaigns to distant places must have made the burden of military service great,[99] and the actual ability to provide the type of service required must have been lacking to many. This fact eventually made itself felt in the law; the kings began to ease the burden of military service from the shoulders of poorer men, the first such concessions being made in 805.[100] Men who had wealth, whether their own or that held as *beneficia*, had to bear the burden of military service more and more.

By the ninth century the Carolingian army had been largely transformed from an infantry to a cavalry army,[101] so that in 864 Charles the Bald called into the army only those men who had a horse or who could procure a horse;[102] and with reference to events in 891, the author of the *Annales Fuldenses* said that the Franks were unaccustomed to fighting on foot.[103] This does not mean that infantry disappeared; but mounted warriors had become the essential part of an army.[104] The shift from infantry to cavalry only accentuated the tendency to make military service the practical responsibility of a smaller and wealthier class; the poor man could not afford the necessary equipment and indeed as a foot soldier he was of less and less value in fighting.[105]

Under such conditions fighting became the career of a restricted class of men. Even though a legal obligation may have rested upon all to aid in the defense of the realm, in practice only certain men found themselves able to acquit themselves of this obligation in a satisfactory manner, and they were recognized as the ones who were the real debtors of military service, men who, equipped with horses, arms, clothing, and food, could go without delay wherever the exigencies of war demanded and who could remain as long as need be.[106]

What is more natural than that men who are capable of such specialized service as this should be taken into commendation to perform a definite function of military character, and so should receive a distinguishing name, the name of "vassal"? Since they are military men and may be used as a bodyguard, individuals who are rich enough to reward them find it useful to surround themselves with vassals to protect themselves and their dependents from the ever growing violence of the times. Hence it is that one finds vassals of bishops, abbots, abbesses, counts, and even royal vassals, as well as of the king. Such military retainers were far from unknown in the Merovingian period; if they were not called vassals, they were designated by a variety of terms such as *satellites, sicarii, pueri, viri fortes*.[107]

II

The great bulk of the Carolingian texts which have to do with vassalage suggest directly or accord with the interpretation which we have just given. There are, however, a few texts which have been used by historians to justify the belief that the term vassal covers more than those men whose special function was to provide military or armed service, that in fact there were included among the vassals bishops, abbots, counts, and other functionaries, and great magnates. We must now turn to these texts to determine if they are in accord with our interpretation of vassalage so far presented or if they make necessary a broader definition.

The first text to consider is the celebrated one with regard to Tassilo. Bavaria had long been a duchy;[108] in the course of the seventh century it became in fact the hereditary possession of the house of the Agilolfings who, although in origin only agents of the Merovingians, really replaced the king even in the law so that they spoke of Bavaria as their *regnum*[109] in which was to be found not the king's peace but the duke's peace.[110] The tradition of Bavarian independence was strong in the first half of the eighth century and it brought about a war in 743 between the duke, Odilo, and his brothers-in-law, Carloman and Pepin, Carolingian mayors; in this war the duke was defeated and lost not his duchy but a strip of territory, the Nordgau.[111]

At Odilo's death in 748 he left his wife Hiltrude, a sister of Pepin, and a young son Tassilo III.[112] Tassilo was deprived momentarily of his duchy by Grifo, Pepin's half-brother and bitter enemy, who had managed to stir up a revolt of the Bavarians in his favor. By 749 the Bavarians had surrendered Grifo to Pepin, who apparently not daring to suppress the duchy at this time, gave it to Tassilo III but under the regency of his mother, Hiltrude, Pepin's own sister.[113] Whether or not the duchy was conceded by Pepin to Tassilo as a *beneficium*,[114] a serious breach had been made in the independence of the duchy. The Bavarians had to swear an oath to Pepin that they would not be rebellious towards him,[115] and Pepin's name appeared in Bavarian charters.[116] In legislative action and administration Bavaria still remained separate from the Frankish kingdom.[117] Hiltrude died in 754 and Tassilo probably began his personal rule at that time. He remained, however, under the influence of his uncle, and went with the latter to Italy in the expedition of 756, a fact which indicated the Frankish hegemony over Bavaria.[118] In May, 757, Pepin "held his *placitum* with the Franks at Compiègne, and there came Tassilo, duke of the Bavarians, who commended himself by hand (*per manus*) into vassalage and who swore many and innumerable oaths; and, placing his hands upon the relics of the saints he promised fidelity to king Pepin and to his sons, lords Charles and Carloman, as a vassal with good intentions and firm devotion to justice, just as a vassal ought to be toward his lords. Tassilo affirmed upon the bodies of the saints, Denis, Rusticus, Eleutherius, Germanus, and Martin, that all the days of his life he would do as he had promised in his oaths; and the more important (*maiores natu*) of his men who were with him confirmed his promise there and in many other places." [119]

How is this to be interpreted? Can it be that Tassilo, a duke, commended himself into the king's service in the inferior capacity of a vassal? Or is this so impossible that "vassal" must mean something other than a military functionary of not too exalted rank?

A debate has recently arisen over this text between Lot and Dumas. The former maintains that this is "un serment vassalique," by which he simply means that Tassilo attached himself to Pepin by the narrow bond of commendation which is the same as vassalage.[120] He is not thinking of vassalage as a particular function in the royal administration as we have interpreted it. Dumas[121] on the other hand argues on our ground; he says that *vassaticum* cannot mean here the position of a vassal, "un grand de seconde classe qui prenait rang après les comtes." He continues, "sérieusement vous n'allez pas soutenir que Tassilon soit réduit à ce rang. Il reste duc de Bavière; il ne tombe pas dans la catégorie des *vassi dominici*. Jusqu'alors prince indépendant, il promet qu'il sera fidèle au roi des Francs comme le serviteur doit l'être envers son maître." Consequently, Dumas prefers to interpret *vassaticum* in this passage as a vague sort of *servitium*. Dumas really admits that Tassilo felt some of the consequences of "vassalage," the necessity to serve a master, and he prefers *servitium* to what the text specifically calls *vassaticum*.

Is it really foolish to give this text its "face value," to maintain that Tassilo acknowledged that he was a servant of Pepin of second rank? Pepin had reason to fear the independence of Bavaria. If Tassilo, its duke, could be made to recognize publicly in some dramatic fashion his subservience to him, the hold of the Franks over Bavaria would be emphasized and made more certain. Tassilo could probably be influenced to do this easily, for he was a boy of fifteen at the time and under the influence of his uncle who had secured this very duchy for him only eight years before. What better way could there be to obtain this desired result than to ask Tassilo to proclaim himself a servant of the king, and not a servant of the highest rank? And then to get the *maiores natu* of Bavaria to recognize this fact? [122]

This commendation of Tassilo must have been regarded as unusual at the time; for it and the arrival of an organ in France are the only two events indicated for 757 by the principal annals of the time, the *Annales Regni Francorum* and the *Annales Einhardi*. This might be explained simply by the fact that the duke of Bavaria had commended himself, but it is significant that the texts say that he commended himself *in vassatico*. Tassilo is the only great magnate of whom it is said that he "commended himself *in vassatico*."[123] Indeed *vassaticum* is used very infrequently. It does not appear in the *Annales Bertiniani* or the *Annales Fuldenses*. The only times that it appears in the *Annales Regni Francorum* or the *Annales Einhardi* are with reference to Tassilo.[124] Its rare appearances in the capitularies have to do with lesser men who might well occupy an inferior position without occasioning surprise.[125] Furthermore, the precision of the statement that Tassilo commended himself *in vassatico* is unusual. The Carolingian writers contented themselves almost exclusively with such statements as this: the bishops, abbots, counts, and vassals commended themselves, adding sometimes, into the hands of the king.[126] These men had entered the service of the king and naturally each one would serve the king according to his function and personal position (*secundum meum ministerium et secundum meam personam*), as their oath of 858 says.[127] The fact that the annalists bothered to put the phrase *in vassatico* after the statement that Tassilo had commended himself, suggests that there was something unusual about his commending himself *into vassalage*. Note the description in the *Annales Einhardi*, how detailed it is: "In accordance with the Frankish custom he commended himself with his own hands into the hands of the king in vassalage and he promised fidelity to king Pepin as well as to his sons Charles and Carloman with an oath sworn over the body of St. Denis; not only that, he also promised with a similar oath over the bodies of St. Martin and St. Germanus that he would preserve his fidelity to his lords all the days of his life."[128] Tassilo commended himself with his own hand into the hands of the king in vassalage. Furthermore, Tassilo did this *more Francico*; whatever Tassilo may be in Bavaria, according to Frankish custom, he had declared himself a vassal of the king. Almost all other descriptions of vassalage set in the *se commendare* form say only that a man has commended himself into the hands of another, but the texts with regard to Tassilo add *in vassatico*.[129] The *Annales Regni Francorum* is particularly insistent upon the fact that Tassilo became a vassal: he commended himself by the hand into *vassalage,* and he promised to be faithful to the king just as a *vassal* with right intentions and firm devotion, just as a *vassal* ought to be to his lord.[130]

A statement made by Tassilo himself contributes to the belief that he was forced to undergo humiliation by declaring himself a dependent of lower rank. By 763 Tassilo had wearied of his subservience to Pepin, and he deserted the latter during a campaign in Aquitaine, swearing that he would never again come to the king.[131] Pepin was too occupied at the time to retaliate, and Tassilo ruled for all practical purposes as an independent prince.[132] By 770 friendlier relations existed between Tassilo and Charlemagne, now king of the Franks,[133] but Tassilo's questionable fidelity was still a worry to the Frankish king. In 781 Charles and the pope each sent two *missi* to Tassilo to urge him to remember the oaths which he had once sworn and not to act except in accord with them. Tassilo, impressed by the successes of Charlemagne in Italy and Saxony,[134] expressed his adherence, and even said that he would come to the king. The offer to appear before Charles apparently came from Tassilo himself, and at this meeting he renewed his oaths and declared that he would keep all his promises given to Pepin; in addition, he gave twelve hostages.[135] It seems significant that in connection with this voluntary action on Tassilo's part, none of the texts say one word about vassalage.[136] Tassilo may have made a number of specific promises, but absolute silence on this point in the annals which had described at length his earlier commendation into vassalage makes it seem quite likely that at this time Tassilo did not declare himself a vassal of Charles.

Trouble continued to crop up between the Franks and the Bavarians and there was much ill-will as well as some bloodshed. By 787 things had reached such a pass that Tassilo, suffering from some misgivings, despatched an embassy to Rome to secure the services of the pope as a mediator between himself and Charlemagne. But the pope was by this time subservient to the Frankish king and Tassilo was told that if he continued to disregard his promises of obedience to Charlemagne, the latter could send an army into Bavaria that would be absolved of all guilt for the bloodshed and injury done during the war. At this juncture Charlemagne ordered Tassilo to follow the pope's advice and to come to him. Tassilo refused, so Charlemagne began an invasion of Bavaria with three armies. Thus menaced on several sides the Bavarians deserted their duke. There was nothing left for Tassilo to do but to yield under compulsion,[137] and *this time* he went to Charles and declared himself a *vassal*. "Pressed on all sides, Tassilo went himself and commended (*tradens*) himself with his hands into the hands of the lord king Charles in vassalage, and he gave back the duchy which had been given (*commissum*) him by the lord king Pepin; and he recognized that he had sinned in all ways and acted badly. Then finally, renewing his oaths, he gave twelve selected hostages and a thirteenth, his son Theodo."[138] Now, "under duress vile" he commends himself with his hands into the hands of the lord king Charles in vassalage, thus again demeaning himself publicly by declaring himself the vassal of Charles.[139]

Tassilo had eaten humble pie, but he did not relish it. In the very next year he came to the king's meeting at Ingelheim at the king's orders "like other vassals of the king."[140] Once there, certain Bavarians loyal to Charles revealed that Tassilo had been treating with the Avars, bitter enemies of the Franks, that he had sought to win over vassals of the king, and that he had ordered the Bavarians to include a mental reservation in their oaths

VASSI 31

of fidelity to Charles; and what is more, that he had said that even if he had ten sons to lose,[141] he would rather lose all than consent to things as they stood, as he had sworn, yes, that it was even better to be dead than so to live.[142] Better to lose ten sons, better indeed to be dead, than what? Than for a duke of Bavaria to consent to the position of a vassal with all the humble connotations which that term might still imply in the eighth century, the position of a *servus* as the author of the *Annales Mettenses* interpreted it,[143] the position which even an unfree man who was given horses and arms by his master might attain to.[144] Apparently that was provocation enough for treason, for treating with the worst enemies of the Franks, the Avars, even if they lay dangerously close to the Bavarians too.

In conclusion, then, we interpret these texts as meaning that the commendation of Tassilo into the relatively inferior position of vassalage was highly unusual, indeed extraordinary when one remembers that the term "vassal" had barely extricated itself from the more completely dependent circumstances of unfree service.[145] It was recognized as an unusual act at the time. Tassilo publicly declared himself an inferior servant of the Frankish king, once when very young and under his uncle's influence and another time when under cruel compulsion, and then he began to take treasonable steps to extricate himself from a situation which he regarded as worse than death and to escape from which he was willing to give the lives of ten sons. The story of Tassilo therefore suggests that a vassal was a servant of so inferior a rank that a great magnate of the realm would not willingly be one. Thus the texts concerning Tassilo's commendation are consonant with the interpretation of vassalage presented earlier. More than that, they serve to reinforce rather than to destroy this interpretation.

A similar conclusion results from the consideration of a text drawn from the Monk of St. Gall, despite the fact that Waitz cited this same text to justify the assertion that royal princes became vassals.[146] The portion quoted by Waitz is a passage where Louis the German says to his father Louis the Pious, "When I was your vassal, I stood behind you with men of my own rank as I was bound to do; but now that I am your colleague and of your rank, I rightly claim equality with you." [147]

This text should never have been quoted separately from the rest of its context.[148] The Monk says: "Since the time has come to make honorable mention of your praiseworthy father [Louis the German], may I recall some prophetic words spoken by the most wise Charles [Charlemagne] about him. When he was *six years old* and had been so carefully reared in the house of his father that he was considered, and not unjustly, wiser than men of sixty, his most loving father, hardly thinking it possible that he could bring him to see his grandfather, nevertheless took him from his mother who had cared for him so tenderly, and began to instruct him in the modest conduct which is proper in the presence of the emperor, telling how he was to answer questions, and how he was in all things to show deference to his father. And so his father took him to the palace, and on the first or second day the emperor [Charlemagne]noticed [the little Louis] among the other courtiers, and said to his son Louis [the Pious], 'Who is that little fellow?' He was answered, 'He is mine, and yours if you wish him.' The Emperor said, 'Give him to me.' When this was done, he kissed the boy and sent him back to where he had been standing. But little Louis,

VASSI

now conscious of his own rank, disdained a position behind the emperor, so he calmly and composedly walked over and stood on equal footing with his father. The prophetic Charles, seeing this, ordered his son Louis to ask the boy why he had acted this way and for what reason he had presumed to act as an equal of his father. He replied with good reason, 'When I was your vassal, I stood behind you with men of my own rank as I was bound to do; but now that I am your fellow and of your rank, I rightly claim equality with you.' When Louis had retold this answer to the emperor, the latter answered in this fashion, 'If that little fellow lives, he will be something great!' "

The legendary quality of this tale is obvious: at the age of six Louis the German renounces his vassalage to his father. One can hardly argue on the basis of this text that Louis the German actually served his father in the capacity of a vassal. The story does seem to indicate, like the case of Tassilo, that a vassal's rank is so inferior that a self-respecting prince would abhor it.

Waitz cites another text from the pen of the Monk of St. Gall as justification for the assertion that higher officials were regarded and designated as vassals.[149] As Waitz cites the text, it reads: "tam bonum vel meliorem vassallum, quam ille comes est aut episcopus." He does not actually translate it, but if it is to justify his statement, it must be translated: "as good or better a vassal as that count or bishop"; therefore, a count or a bishop is a vassal.

Let us place this text in its full context.[150] The Monk of St. Gall states that Charlemagne did not give to any of his counts except those on the frontiers more than one *comitatus*, nor did he ever give to any of his bishops except in very special cases a monastery or churches pertaining to the royal right. The writer was not thinking of the bishoprics as comprised in the term *aecclesia*; for if he were, the passage could then read that Charles gave bishoprics to none of his bishops save in certain cases, which would be an absurdity. He must have been thinking rather of the lands with which certain foundations at the king's disposal had been endowed; the king did not give these to bishops because they already had at their disposal the lands attached to their bishoprics, and so already had material reasons for being devoted to the king. Nor was the writer thinking of the office of count. From the expressions which follow, "cum illo fisco vel curte, illa abbateiola vel aecclesia," we see that he means the lands which might be given to the count as a reward for his services. Possibly a count might be charged with the function of administering a second county but presumably his recompense would not ordinarily be doubled. Rather the revenue and lands attached to the office of count in the second county would be given to other men. When Charles was asked by his counsellors why he did not give these lands to the count or the bishop, he replied that with that land or revenue, with that small monastery or church, he could make faithful to him just as good or better a vassal as So-and-so (who already held the lands of one county or bishopric) was a count or bishop (*cum illo fisco vel curte, illa abbateiola vel aecclesia, tam bonum vel meliorem vassallum, quam ille comes est aut episcopus, fidelem mihi facio.*)

The Monk of St. Gall did not express himself clearly and this translation is just as possible grammatically as the translation of Waitz, that is, "as good or better a vassal as that count or bishop." The former accords if anything better with the general sense of the passage than the latter. This text therefore should not be used as positive evidence for either a possible broad interpretation of vassalage or for the narrow interpretation which we have so far presented; nor does it have any strong negative force against either interpretation.

There are two texts in the *Annales Laureshamenses* which permit a broader interpretation of vassalage. In one the annalist informs us that Charlemagne was merciful toward the poor folk of his realm, so that he was unwilling to send forth from the palace *pauperiores vassos suos* for the doing of justice on account of gifts.[151] The construction of this sentence could be clearer, but the annalist seems to mean that Charlemagne did not send out as judges poorer men who might be more susceptible to bribes. The annalist continues, saying that Charlemagne chose rather archbishops, bishops, and abbots along with dukes and counts, men who had no need to receive gifts on behalf of innocent folk; these men he sent throughout his realm to bring justice to churches, widows, orphans, the poor, and all the people. The question which concerns us has to do with the *pauperiores vassos suos*. When the annalist says that Charlemagne sent out as judges not his poorer vassals but rather his archbishops, bishops, and abbots along with dukes and counts, does he mean to imply that archbishops, bishops, abbots along with dukes and counts are vassals, different from the *vassos* mentioned previously only in that they are richer and less susceptible to bribery? Such an interpretation is grammatically possible. But it should also be observed that the *pauperiores vassos suos* is quite far removed from the *archiepiscopos et reliquos episcopos et abbates cum ducibus et comitibus* and the annalist may not have had in mind a genuine comparison between the two groups. He might have meant only that the king did not send out "poorer men, his vassals" or "quite poor men, his vassals."

In the second text in the *Annales Laureshamenses* which permits a broader interpretation of vassalage the annalist says that in 799 Charlemagne carried off a number of Saxons with their wives and children and settled them in Frankish territory. Then, "ipsam terram eorum divisit inter fideles suos, id est episcopos, presbyteros, comites et alios vassos suos."[152] There is no disputing that this may grammatically be interpreted to mean that he divided the land of the Saxons among his faithful servants, that is, bishops, priests, counts, and others of his vassals; the *alios* then refers to bishops, priests, and counts who thus are included among the vassals, and who are in some sense vassals along with other men who are just vassals and nothing more.

It is also equally true that this text can be interpreted to mean that he divided the land among his *fideles*, that is, bishops, priests, counts, and other *fideles*, namely his vassals; in other words, the *alios* refers back to the *fideles* rather than to the bishops, priests, and counts, or any one of them. The *id est* lends its testimony to this: the author is going to explain to what *fideles* land was given, and this is what is paramount in his mind, so that the *alios* preferably refers to the *fideles*. There is nothing in the least surprising in this interpretation; we shall demonstrate presently that the vassals are among the *fideles*. This text then is of neither a positive nor a negative character; it can accord with either a broad or a narrow interpretation of vassalage.[153]

However, a text, very similar to this one of the *Annales Laureshamenses*, unquestionably supports the narrow interpretation of vassalage. It is in the *Vita Hludowici Imperatoris*, c. 3.[154] Charlemagne established in Aquitaine "comites, abbates, necnon alios plurimos quos vassos vulgo vocant, ex gente Francorum, quorum prudentiae et fortitudini nulli calliditate nulli vi obviare fuerit tutum, eisque commisit curam regni prout utile iudicavit, finium tutamen, villarumque regiarum ruralem provisionem." We have here to do with a careful writer of Latin. The word *vassus* was not yet part of good literary Latin; the writer felt that he had to make a slight apology for using it, so he said that it was a word of common use (*quos vassos vulgo vocant*); and then he explained that they were men before whom it was not safe to show any hot temper or resistance. The *vassos* does not apply to the *comites* and *abbates*, but only to the *alios plurimos*, for an inspection of the grammar shows that the writer constructed his sentence so as to leave no ambiguity on this score. The *quos* should properly refer to the *alios plurimos* which directly precedes it, rather than to *comites* or *abbates* or both; *quorum*, the same relative, introduces a clause which refers back to the same noun, the *alios plurimos*, though it could also refer to *vassos* without changing the meaning in the least. When the writer wished to refer to all three groups who were entrusted with the care of the realm, the frontiers, and royal lands, he switched to a different pronoun, namely *eis*, thereby making his meaning quite clear. Therefore, the many men other than counts and abbots were the men commonly called vassals before whom it was unsafe to show any hot temper or resistance.

A comparison of the sentence from the *Vita Hludowici Imperatoris* (1) with that from the *Annales Laureshamenses* (2) gives further support to the interpretation of the Lorsch text along the lines just described.

1. Ordinavit autem per totam Aquitaniam
2. Terram divisit inter fideles suos, id est

1. abbates   comites necnon alios plurimos
2. episcopos,presbyteros,comites,   et   alios

1. quos vassos vulgo vocant.
2.   vassos suos.

In the case of (1) we know that the writer was not thinking of abbots and counts as vassals. In the case of (2) there are two possibilities, in accordance with which the writer would not have been thinking of bishops, priests, and counts as vassals just as the writer of (1) did not think of counts and abbots as vassals. One possibility is that the *alios* of (2) refers back specifically to *fideles*; Charlemagne divided the lands among his faithful servants (*fideles*), that is, bishops, priests, counts, and other *fideles*, (that is) his vassals. The other possibility is that the *alios*, just like the *alios* in (1), does not refer back specifically to any of the foregoing; Charlemagne divided the lands among his faithful servants, that is, bishops, priests, counts, and others, his vassals. This latter interpretation of the text involves only the insertion of a comma. If in spite of the existence of these possibilities by which the two may be reconciled, one would assert that the writer of the *Annales Laureshamenses* included bishops, priests, and counts among the vassals, then it must be admitted that his testimony is opposed by that of the writer of the *Vita Hludowici Imperatoris* who did not include abbots and counts among the vassals.

Another possibility, however, is that the annalist of Lorsch used the term *vassus* very loosely, applying it to a wider category than that of armed retainers. The case of Witzin demonstrates this possibility. This Slavic chief first appears in the *Annales Regni Francorum* under the year 789. In that year Charlemagne brought under his domination the Slavic tribe of the Wilzi or Welatabi by leading into their region an army composed of Franks, Saxons, Frisians, and Slavs including the Sorabi and the Abodriti whose prince was Witzin.[155] The only other deed of Witzin which history remembers is his death in 795. Charles in that year had marched into Saxony and he was awaiting at Lüne the arrival of Witzin and the Abodriti. There he learned that the Saxons had killed Witzin while the latter was on his way to Charles. In this connection the *Annales Laureshamenses* refers to Witzin as "vassum domni regis Wizzin regem Abotridarum."[156] The annalist thus speaks of him as a *king* and as a *vassal* of Charlemagne. This is the only text in which Witzin is called a vassal.[157] He figures in the *Annales Regni Francorum*, the *Annales Einhardi*, the *Annales Sithienses*, the *Annales Fuldenses Einhardi*, the *Annales Mosellani*, the *Annales Petaviani*, and the *Poeta Saxo*. In not one of these is he called a vassal of Charles, though of course he recognized the superiority of the Frankish king. More than that, these writers are not agreed among themselves as to what he should be called. The *Annales Regni Francorum* in 789[158] called him *princeps* of the Abodriti; in 795 they called him *rex* as did the *Annales Einhardi*, the *Poeta Saxo*, the *Annales Laureshamenses*, the *Annales Mosellani*. But according to the *Annales Sithienses*, the *Annales Fuldenses Einhardi*, and the *Annales Petaviani* he was *dux*.[159] Obviously, none of these terms correspond actually to their Frankish parallels, for Witzin did not fall within the regular official hierarchy of the Frankish government. Who was Witzin? He was the chief of a tribe of Slavs living to the east beyond the Saxons, who found it convenient to be an ally of Charlemagne against a common enemy who lay between him and the Franks. He was not charged with an institutionalized administrative office under the control of the Frankish king. The ordinary terms did not fit him. Indeed, it may be that we are maligning the Lorsch annalist in suggesting that he was eccentric in his use of the term vassal. It was the military help of the Abodriti that Charlemagne expected,[160] and it need not be regarded as surprising that he called this military ally who fell outside the normal framework of the Frankish administration a "vassal."

The *Aldrici Episcopi Cenomannici Memoriale* in the *Gesta Aldrici*[161] provides a text somewhat similar to the second text cited from the *Annales Laureshamenses*. In a dispute between the bishop of Le Mans and the abbot of St. Calais, Louis the Pious "ordered an inquest by Ebroin, bishop of Poitiers, and Erchinradus, bishop of Paris, and Rorigo, count, and Altmarus, seneschal of the empress and a palatine *missus, una cum aliis vassis dominicis.*" Here again, grammatically the *aliis* could refer to all the inquisitors, so that we would have the bishops, count, and seneschal all *vassi dominici*. But this interpretation even those who believe in a broad definition of vassalage as well as a narrow would probably not be willing to admit; for they conceive of those who are vassals and nothing more, that is, not also bishops or abbots or counts, as *vassi dominici*.[162] Grammatically it is possible that the *aliis* does not refer back to any of the foregoing. In this case the text would mean that the king sent as inquisitors, the two bishops, the count, and the seneschal along with others, men who were his vassals (*vassi dominici*); this does not imply at all that the bishops, counts, or seneschal were *vassi dominici*.

Grammatically, the *aliis* could refer back also to the last man mentioned, Altmarus, seneschal of the queen and a palatine *missus*. Granting this, we are not forced to recognize a broad usage in this instance for it would not be surprising if one of the queen's household officers [163] could at the same time serve as a royal vassal. In fact, an occasional combination of the function of vassal with that of another servant may well have occurred without the identity of the two functions being lost. The same *Memoriale* indicates among a list of judges *Fulco vassus dominicus et comes palatii* and *Ragenarius vassus dominicus et comes palatii*,[164] vassals who are also palace counts. However, the pedigree of the *Memoriale* itself must be taken into account. The *Memoriale* [165] purports to have been written at Aachen, May 1, 838, and to describe the procedure by which Louis the Pious restored to the church of Le Mans its rights over the monastery of St. Calais. At Verberie in 863 the diplomas presented by Robert, bishop of Le Mans, as evidence of his rights over the monastery were declared forgeries and St. Calais was taken from him. Modern scholars have generally concurred in this opinion. Roth, Sickel, Mühlbacher, and Simson all regarded these diplomas including the *Memoriale* as forgeries.[166] At first Julien Havet was of the same opinion; [167] later he decided that all these diplomas were authentic.[168] His argument was not convincing, and Mühlbacher continued to regard the *Memoriale* as a forgery.[169] Werminghoff likewise placed it among spurious acts.[170]

Even if the *Memoriale* is a forgery, it falls within the Carolingian period and must be considered. The possible interpretations of the *aliis* clause contained in it have already been discussed, and the question of authenticity is not of any particular significance with regard to it. Even if the *Memoriale* were authentic, the text with the *aliis* clause may still be in accord with the narrow interpretation of vassalage. The question of authenticity is of greater moment with regard to Fulco and Ragenarius, the *comites palatii* who are also called vassals. Even if we assume that the *Memoriale* has all the validity of an official act, the weight of the evidence for the narrow interpretation of vassalage plus the fact that this is the only place where *comites palatii*, or counts of any kind, are unmistakably called vassals, could lead to the conclusion that this case represents a highly unusual combination of two different functions generally kept separate. On the other hand, the probability of forgery causes one to wonder if such a combination of *comes palatii* and *vassus dominicus* ever actually took place. Simson called attention to the fact that there is no mention of a Fulco and Ragenarius as *comites palatii* in any source save the *Gesta Aldrici*, and that the forger used *comites palatii* with the greatest liberality.[171] Fulco and Ragenarius may both be inventions of the forger; however, the forger must have thought that a *comes palatii* might at the same time be a vassal. But since the *Memoriale* is probably a forgery by a private person and not a *bona fide* document drawn up by the king's agents, it must be admitted that the evidence for a combination of the functions of *comes palatii* and a vassal in this, the only case, is not of any official character and may not actually have occurred at all.

There are two certain instances of vassals who at the same time held other positions. Waitz called attention to a diploma of Louis II of Italy in which there appears "A. vassus et ministeriale domni regis"[172] and to another diploma of the same king for "Salamannus, dilectus vassus noster, abba monasterii" of Pfävers in Switzerland.[173] The fact that the double functions of vassal and *ministerialis*, and of vassal and abbot are carefully designated shows only that the two functions were different, even though in certain rare instances they might be exercised by the same man.

The last debatable text which we shall consider is a passage in the *Vita Walae* (*Epitaphium Arsenii*) of Radbertus Paschasius concerning events just preceding the deposition of Louis the Pious at the hands of his sons in 833. Radbert says that the father sent to his sons certain *capitula* with regard to the quarrel between them.[174] First he urged them to remember that they were his sons. To this the sons replied that they held nothing dearer in life than their father, that they came to him humbly, devotedly, obediently under his command as was proper; that they were not in revolt against him as it was alleged by men hostile to them, who wished to ruin them; but that as suppliants they asked his grace, indulgence, and mercy. Then in another *capitulum* Louis said, "Remember also that you are my vassals and that you have affirmed your good faith [175] to me with an oath" (*mementote, inquit, etiam quod mei vasalli estis, mihique cum iuramento fidem firmastis.*) To this the sons answered that they cherished what he had commanded since they were faithful because of the responsibility imposed upon them by nature, by their promises, and by every sacrament of the true faith. Therefore, just as they had never deserted his service, so in the future as long as life lasted, they would never desert him.

It should be noted that the sons recognize that they are in the service of their father; they claim that they have never deserted his service and never will. As vassals of course they would be in his service. But can it be that the sons of the king were vassals and that this means that they served him as soldiers and functionaries not of the very highest rank? It may be so; if so, however, only of the sons of Louis the Pious is it ever said that they were the king's vassals.[176] This may therefore be an exceptional case; it is hardly sufficient evidence for us to assert that it was the general practice for the king's sons to serve him as vassals.

However, this may be granting more than is necessary. Were these words ever spoken by Louis the Pious and his sons or are they the product of Radbert's imagination? It was Simson's opinion that we owe them to the fantasy of Radbert, a persistent champion of Wala and therefore a detractor of Louis the Pious. Simson called attention to the fact that the remarks quoted from Louis are very brief whereas the justification of their conduct presented by the sons was quoted at length. Furthermore, Simson saw in the speeches certain similarities to the writings of Radbert himself which made him think that Radbert actually forged the speeches.[177] It may be noted in support of Simson's contention that the general effect of the whole passage is to justify the conduct of the sons at the expense of the father and that the sentence with which we are concerned may be interpreted as especially helpful in their defense. Radbert did not quote Louis in the entirety. In the first exchange he did not even quote Louis directly: "Primum rememorari eos monet, quod filii eius sint, et ipse eos Deo auctore genuerit." Then following a long answer by the sons, Radbert made a choice, it would seem, from the statements of Louis, for he says: "*Deinde in alio capitulo*" and then quotes the statement of Louis that his sons are his vassals. Supposing that Radbert forged this passage, does anything lie behind his selection of these words? Possibly so. Note what Radbert says just before he begins this series of quotations, that "according to the law of God, of nature, and of the land it has been written, 'Sons, obey your father,' [178] and 'Fathers, do not provoke your sons to anger.' [179] If these commands had been carefully kept on both sides, so much misfortune would not have occurred." [180] What better way to justify the sons' conduct than to choose a remark of the father which would move the sons to a just anger, than to show that the father called his sons his *vassals*, that he expected them, princes royal, to hold the rank of an inferior functionary? Had Radbert chosen to write this himself, that is, to invent these conversations, his chances of detection were slight; he was writing at least twenty years after these events had taken place and Louis the Pious was long dead.[181]

It is possible that Simson was doing Radbert an injustice when he believed him to be a forger; the honesty of Radbert in this matter was defended by Rodenberg, who thought that this interchange of conversation might have been copied from a manifesto or proclamation published by the sons.[182] Dümmler recognized that Radbert, zealous partisan of Wala, is the only one on whose authority we have this conversation,[183] but said that there is no conclusive evidence for rejecting this conversation, for it is not improbable that Radbert had access to a proclamation issued by the sons.[184]

It is impossible to come to a certain judgment with regard to this text. It may be a forgery designed to show that the father had moved his sons to a just anger by insisting that they were merely his vassals, servants of inferior rank; it may be genuine in which case we observe that it is only these royal sons who were vassals; in either case their vassalage can be interpreted in the narrow sense. It is also possible, if this remark is genuine, that Louis the Pious meant a broader kind of vassalage; what this vassalage would be is not really indicated for even the narrow vassalage involved an affirmation of fidelity on oath and the performance of service.[185] Perhaps Louis the Pious was thinking of the term "vassal" not in the sense typical of the ninth century but in the original general meaning of an unfree servant; in an effort to impress upon his sons the necessity of their being obedient to him, he may have chosen for the purpose of emphasis a word used in the archaic sense of an unfree servant.[186]

We have now reviewed the evidence upon which the case for the broad interpretation of vassalage could be based. What conclusions can one draw from it? In the first place, none of it is of a completely positive character, none of it excludes anything but a broad interpretation. That which most favors this interpretation is the quotation by Radbertus Paschasius of the injunction of Louis the Pious to his sons to remember that they were his vassals; but there is always the possibility that this was part of a forgery by Radbert to justify the sons' conduct.

As analysis has shown, the other texts *can* be interpreted in accord with either the narrow or the broad interpretation. In the texts with *alios* clauses it is only by inference that one can conclude that their authors actually thought of bishops, priests, and counts as vassals; but it is also possible to interpret these texts so that one does not infer a broad meaning of vassals. The same is to be said of the Monk of St. Gall's story of Charlemagne's policy with regard to the lands given to counts and bishops.

If it were accepted as true that all great magnates who commended themselves to the king were among the king's vassals, there would be no reason for not supposing that the case of Witzin would be in accord with this practice. But there is no sufficient reason to deny that the case of Witzin could accord with the narrow interpretation of vassalage. It was his military help which was expected, and we are not certain enough of his actual position to assert that it would be incongruous for him to be a "real" vassal.

Two *comites palatii* (in a ninth-century forgery) and a *ministerialis* were called *vassi*. This can be explained on the grounds that in these rare cases one and the same man was vested with two separate functions. Hence these texts can be interpreted in accord with the narrow meaning as well as the broad. One cannot argue from these cases that *comites palatii* and *ministeriales* were always or were usually vassals. No one would argue for a special status for abbots in this period, yet the main case for the inclusion of the abbots among the vassals must rest upon the single case of Salomannus who was abbot of Pfävers and also a vassal of the king. If this were sufficient proof, one would be equally justified in asserting that counts were doorkeepers, for we know that Agbertus, a count, was also a doorkeeper.[187]

The case of Tassilo *can* be read either way. However, it is far more probable that it favors the narrow interpretation, for it points to the conclusion that the position of a vassal was one more humble than that ordinarily held by a duke. Such a conclusion is compatible with the narrow interpretation of vassalage and not with the broad interpretation. The Monk of St. Gall's story about the six-year-old Louis the German points for a similar reason toward the narrow interpretation.

Even if several or all of these doubtful texts should be understood as using the term vassal in a broad sense, there would still be the possibility that these texts are then only instances of loose usage rather than evidence that magnates in general were vassals. In these cases the use of vassal may hark back to the original meaning of a household servant without the martial connotations generally characteristic of the term in the Carolingian period. These possible cases of loose usage in the Carolingian period occur in a few scattered literary sources and none of them are found in the most important official sources of the period; every mention of vassalage in the capitularies accords with the narrow interpretation. It is not possible to organize these instances of a possible broad usage in such a way as to assert that a new usage was developing as time passed.[188] Throughout the period under consideration here the meaning of vassalage seems to have remained constant. It seems very dangerous, then, on the basis of such dubious texts to erect a theory that higher state functionaries were vassals and to conclude that where a text says *se commendare* one can presuppose *se commendare in vassaticum*. The main reason for deciding against such a theory, however, is that a solid and overwhelming body of evidence stands in opposition to it and points to the conclusion that *vassi* were distinguished from other functionaries; that *vassi* were in fact of lower rank than bishops, abbots, and counts; that *vassaticum* had a connotation which was inappropriate or inadequate for bishops, priests, abbots, and even counts, namely, that of the position of a fighting man. Those texts which seem to go beyond this limited meaning of the term *vassus* are not numerous, are not unambiguous, and can be explained in ways which leave the limitation in effect as a general principle. All the weight of probability is on the side of the theory which is here advanced, and the textual evidence which does not support it is not capable of overthrowing it.

There is evidence other than that which has already been indicated, which argues against the theory that bishops, abbots, and counts were generally regarded as in some sense vassals. No one denies that there were vassals who were neither bishops, abbots, nor counts. On the other hand if bishops, abbots, and counts were regularly vassals, we should expect to find an adjective applied to the word vassal to distinguish or to particularize those vassals who were *not* bishops, abbots, and counts. The logical need for such a qualifying adjective if one starts with such an assumption is proved by the fact that modern historians of such opinion have had to talk about "real" vassals and vassals "proprement dits." But what qualifying adjectives are applied to vassals in the sources? Sometimes they are *vassi dominici, vassalli regii, vassalli imperiales*,[189] the lord's (king's) vassals, the king's vassals, the emperor's vassals. There is absolutely nothing in these adjectives to indicate that they do not include *all* the king's vassals, that there are royal vassals who are not royal vassals but the king's vassals of another kind. In fact, they point in the opposite direction; they mean men who are the king's vassals as opposed to men who are *not* the king's vassals but the vassals of somebody else. For example, in the capitularies the king orders that "our vassals (*vassi nostri*) and the vassals of the bishops, abbots, abbesses, and the counts who were not in the army the preceding year shall pay a fine."[190] Those men who are not "our vassals" are the vassals of other men. *Vassi nostri*, used in contrast to other functionaries,[191] argues likewise against the inclusion of bishops, abbots, and counts among the vassals. There is no indication in the sources of any terms which might be used to separate "real" vassals from a supposed larger group of vassals; and that is the case for the very good reason that the only vassals generally thought of at this time were the "real" vassals.

CHAPTER III

FIDELES

WE HAVE seen in the preceding chapter that despite the frequent practice of modern historians the term "vassal" was not used in Carolingian times to comprise the large group of royal servants who had commended themselves to the king. What term or terms, if any, were used to cover this category of men?

Persons familiar with the literature on commendation will think immediately of a term which is frequently used as a synonym for this act, "homage," and of the word from which it is derived, *homo*. This latter word has a wide variety of uses in the Carolingian period. In its broadest usage it means "man" in the generic sense, as when Charlemagne forbids the burning of a man's (*homo*) body,[192] or calls upon every man (*homo*) in the kingdom to swear the oath of fidelity,[193] or upon every Frankish man to do the same.[194] Or Louis the Pious proclaims that every free man (*homo*) who does not have a seignior has the right to commend himself to whichever of the king's sons he wishes.[195] Since Roman times, however, *homo* has been applied to a somewhat narrower category than generic man; in this use its basic meaning is one who is under the control of another, one who is dependent upon the will of another. It is applied to men whose actual degree of dependency upon a lord varies considerably.[196] Slaves, servants, clients,[197] and dependents such as tenants of wealthy landowners[198] are spoken of as *homines*; so too are men who have commended themselves,[199] who have entered the service of another.[200]

A man who is received into service (*susceptus*) can be spoken of as the *homo* of the man who has received him. An interesting passage in the *Actus Pontificum* of Le Mans illustrates this well. Bishop Gauziolenus in the course of a long and violent episcopacy had given many benefices from the property of his church to men of evil character. Among them was his vidame Abraham who held the monastery of Saint Pierre de la Boisselière. Abraham had behaved scandalously, doing his very best to disperse the monks already attached to his monastery and to prevent the addition of any new members to the congregation. But now, in 770, his protector Gauziolenus was dead, so Abraham "called together his fellows, clerics as well as laymen, and advised them to go to lord Charles, king of the Franks, and to become his *homines*, and so through his gift they would retain their benefices. They yielded to the temptations of human cupidity and followed his advice. Well provided with gold and silver and noble vestments they came to the aforesaid king of the Franks, the most glorious Charles, and petitioned him to permit them to become his *homines*. The king, misled by too human cupidity, *received them (suscepit eos)*, and of his bounty permitted them to have their benefices. Thus he allowed these *homines* of Gauziolenus *whom he had now received into his own service*, to hold as they had held before the monasteries and priories, the lands and manors, which bishops were wont to hold for their work and for the adorning and rebuilding of Holy Church and for rescuing the poor and for supporting the canons and other servants of God." [201] Thus, the men who had been received by Charlemagne into his service had become his *homines*. Other passages show this same use of *homo* for a man received into service through commendation. For example, Rimbert, archbishop of Hamburg (865-888), old and afflicted with foot trouble, had chosen as his assistant the monk Adalgarius who, when Rimbert was incapacitated, performed such episcopal duties as making tours of inspection of the diocese, going to *placita*, or when it was necessary, going with his following on military expeditions or to the royal *palatium*. Finally, Rimbert arranged the confirmation of the election of Adalgarius to succeed himself, and caused him *to be taken into the king's hands* as his *homo* and to be placed among the king's counsellors.[202] This is a clear reference to the use of the hands in the ceremony of commendation. A similar reference to commendation occurs in connection with Zwentibaldus, duke of the Moravians; he was made the *homo* of Charles the Fat in the customary way, *per manus*, and he swore an oath of fidelity.[203]

The term *homo* may be applied to both laymen and clerics; both were included among the *homines* of Gauziolenus who became the *homines* of the king. The term is also applied not only to these men of relatively low status, but also to men of high station such as Adalgarius, archbishop of Hamburg, and Zwentibaldus, duke of the Moravians.

Waitz goes farther than the evidence permits when he says that *homines* are *armed* men in the service of the king [204] or vassals.[205] That *homines* can be armed servants is not to be denied,[206] but to assert that *homines* and armed men (vassals) are *gleichbedeutend*, that is, that all *homines* are armed men, is to assert too much. We have seen that clerics and a bishop are included among the *homines* and they cannot be called armed servants. The most that we can assert is that *homines* may be men who have commended themselves into the service of another; the term does not indicate the exact nature of the services performed.

Men, whether clerical or lay, who serve seigniors other than the king may be called *homines*. We have already encountered the *homines* of Gauziolenus who became in time the king's men. A capitulary issued by Lothair I in 825 refers to *homines* who have commended themselves to seigniors who are vassals of the king.[207] Perhaps to distinguish the *homines* who commend themselves into service from the lesser dependents who might also be called *homines*, the adjective *liberi* was sometimes added. In a passage which clearly contrasts those who have commended themselves to the king with those in turn who commended themselves to the king's *commendati*, Lothair speaks of the latter group as *liberi homines*.[208]

While the term *homines* is frequently found in Carolingian sources to indicate men who serve private seigniors other than the king, its use for men in the king's own service is relatively infrequent. It was left for another word to fill this breach, to be the word ordinarily used to cover the wide group of royal servitors of various kinds. This word was *fideles*.

This term appears in almost every royal diploma and it can be found countless times in the capitularies. It is used occasionally in a broad way as the category which includes all who are under the rule of the king, in other words, all the king's subjects, all those who are faithful to the Holy Church of God and to the king.[209] There is also a narrower use of the term which has been recognized by some historians;[210] the *fideles* may be a much narrower group of men who actually approach the king and who serve him. However, the measure of recognition which has been given to this term has not been sufficient to unseat the term "vassal" in its common modern use. We have already demonstrated the inappropriateness of the term "vassal" for the general category of royal servants. It seems desirable to show further the claim of the term *fideles* to the place denied the term *vassi*.

Many texts suggest a connection between service and the *fideles*. To those *fideles* who have *served* him faithfully and devotedly the king gives rewards.[211] The granting of rewards to *fideles* is, in fact, intended to make them the more ready and faithful in rendering service.[212] Diplomas frequently indicate that a *fidelis* is being rewarded because of his faithful service (*propter fidele servitium*).[213] The king expects his *fideles* to show him respect and proper obedience, to be of assistance to him, and to do for him whatever lies in their power.[214] It is with the help of the *fideles* that the king issues the capitularies for the governance of the mass of his subjects (*populus*). For example, Charles the Bald decrees "that there should remain in force the capitularies which our grandfather and father established for the maintenance and protection of the Holy Church of God and its ministers, and for preserving to the people (*populus*) peace and justice; and there should also remain in force the capitularies which we have established together with our brother kings and with their and our *fideles*."[215] Thus, the people at large, the subjects, are the *populus*; the smaller group of *maiores*[216] who aid the kings in issuing royal capitularies are the *fideles*. These latter men are described in the very same capitulary as the *fideles* who are obedient (*obedientes*) to the command of their seignior (*senior*), who are his true assistants (*adiutores*) and helpers (*cooperatores*), and who render counsel and assistance (*consilio et auxilio*) in accordance with their function and their person (*iuxta suum ministerium et personam*), their knowledge and their ability (*secundum suum scire et posse*), and the ordinances of God and man (*secundum Deum ac secundum seculum*), just as they ought to be towards their king and seignior.[217]

The connection between the term *fideles* and the idea of service is shown particularly well in the oaths taken by the *fideles*. The *fidelis* promises to be a faithful helper (*fidelis adiutor*) with counsel and aid (*consilio et auxilio*) and in accordance with his function and his person (*secundum meum ministerium et secundum meam personam*).[218] The aid and counsel promised the king by the *fidelis* who serves him is to be contrasted with the promise made to him by the ordinary subject who swears in his oath only to be faithful (*fidelis*) insofar as he knows how (*secundum meum savirum*).[219] He does not promise in addition to give aid and counsel. The failure of the subject to promise all that the servant pledges is easily explained. The advice of the ordinary subject would be of little value and his aid of negligible importance. Little more than loyalty could be required of him: he could hardly be helpful in a material way and there would be little point in asking for what he could not give.[220]

In Carolingian times men entered service by commending themselves. If *fidelis* is used for a man who is in service, one would expect to see a connection between *fidelis* and commendation. We find, indeed, that *fidelis* is used to designate a man who has commended himself. This usage is clearly illustrated in the account of the commendation to Louis the Pious of Harold, dispossessed king of the Danes. The latter gave into the hands of Louis "himself and the realm which was rightly his. 'Receive me, Caesar,' he said, 'and the realm which has been

FIDELES

torn from me; of my own free will I put myself at your service.' Caesar took his hands in his own upright hands, and thus the Danish realm was added to that of the righteous Franks. In accordance with Frankish custom, Caesar then gave him a horse and arms, and endowed Harold *now his faithful servant* (*iamque fidelem*) with riches."[221] Having commended himself to the king, he was now the king's *fidelis*.

A charter of Charlemagne dating from 795 demonstrates the same usage. A certain John has come to the king bearing from the king's son, Louis the Pious, a letter which tells how the same John has been responsible for a notable victory over the Saracens. The letter further informs the king that Louis has assigned the manor of Fontes to John and has sent him to the king. The charter goes on to say that after John had presented Louis' letter, he commended himself into the king's hands, and now his faithful servant (*iam dictus fidelis noster Johannes*) John has asked the king to concede to him the manor in question.[222] It is not until *after* the commendation has taken place that Charlemagne's charter refers to John as *fidelis noster*. The two previous references to John in the charter mention only his name.[223] Thus, John became Charlemagne's *fidelis* by commendation into the king's hands.[224]

In still another way there is revealed the connection between *fideles* and the relationship established by commendation. One who receives a man into commendation is called a *senior*. It appears that the man who commends himself may be called a *fidelis*. Implicit in this relationship then is the idea that the man who has commended himself is the *fidelis* of a *senior*. The validity of this hypothesis is attested by the existence of a text containing the phrase *fideles senioris*.²²⁵ The *senior* does actually have *fideles*.

It may be noted in passing that the use of the word *fidelis* for one in service is consistent whether the person receiving the service is a "private" seignior ²²⁶ or the king. The use of *fideles* for the king's servants, however, is more common than that of *homines* which seems to have been used preferably for non-royal servants.

We have already observed that the Carolingian king is not merely a ruler over all his subjects; he is also, so far as certain persons are concerned, a master who receives honorable service. Accordingly he is referred to sometimes as king (*rex*) or lord king (*dominus rex*)²²⁷ but he is also called on occasion king and seignior (*rex et senior*)²²⁸ or lord king and seignior (*dominus rex et senior*.)²²⁹ If the ruler happens to bear the imperial title, he may be called emperor and seignior (*imperator et senior*.)²³⁰ He may also be called prince and seignior (*princeps et senior*).²³¹ The king then is a lord or seignior who has men in his service. We shall now demonstrate 1) that various categories of royal servants are called *fideles* and 2) that these same men commend themselves to the king. In this way the connection between *fideles* and commendation will be further substantiated.

The term *fideles* is applied not only to laymen but also to the clergy. Hincmar of Rheims refers to the oath of the *fidelis* which "we *fideles* of the king, bishops and others of the lay order" swore at Kiersy in 858.²³² Charles the Fat mentions in a diploma of 885 "our *fidelis* Arnaldus, who is now bishop of Toul." ²³³ In addition to bishops, abbots and abbesses are included among the *fideles*.²³⁴

If we turn to the lay officials, we find that even dukes are listed among the *fideles*.²³⁵ Counts are among the *fideles*.[236] Charles the Bald in one and the same diploma refers to Vivianus as "our *fidelis* Vivianus, count" and as "our *fidelis* Vivianus."[237] When the monastery of Saint Lomer le Moutier burned, its charters were destroyed; the abbot requested Charles the Bald to draw up a confirmation of the monastery's possessions. Charles wrote the abbot to ask for the names of the counties in which the monastery had possessions, so that he could inform his *fideles* who were counts in those counties that the monastery's lands were under royal protection.[238] Vassals are likewise among the *fideles*. Charlemagne speaks in a diploma of "our *fideles*," that is, certain counts and vassals.[239] Louis the Pious speaks of Bavo as "our vassal" and also as "our *fidelis*."[240] Charles the Bald refers to "Teodtfredus our vassal" as "our *fidelis*,"[241] and speaks also of "our *fideles*, Vido, Odbertus, *etc*. . . . our vassals."[242] Finally, vicars, *centenarii*,[243] and other unspecified persons, presumably lesser officials, are named among the *fideles*.[244]

Thus, there are designated as *fideles* a wide variety of officials including bishops, abbots, abbesses, dukes, counts, vassals, vicars, *centenarii*, and others. If we have rightly understood the nature of the *fideles*, we should expect to find these various classes of men who are included among the *fideles* commending themselves to the king. We find, in fact, that these men enter the service of their seignior in the usual way: commendation to which the oath of fidelity may be joined.[245]

The ordinary members of the royal administration already found listed among the *fideles* are, as we should expect, found commending themselves. When Louis the Pious set aside a kingdom for Charles the Bald in 837, abbots, counts, and royal vassals commended themselves to Charles and promised fidelity on oath.[246] At the council of Ponthion in 876 five abbots recognized on oath Charles the Bald as their seignior,[247] and in a *placitum* held at Pavia shortly before in the same year, one abbot, one duke, and ten counts had acknowledged him on oath to be their seignior.[248] One may infer from this fact that they had commended themselves. In 863 the duke of Brittany commended himself to Charles the Bald and swore fidelity.[249]

Royal servants referred to by a more general term rather than by definite administrative titles are found commending themselves. In 877 the abbots, *primores* of the realm, and the royal vassals commended themselves to Louis II, son of Charles the Bald, and promised fidelity on oath in the customary fashion.[250] *Primores* had commended themselves to Charles the Bald by giving their hands to him and had sworn fidelity to him [251] when his portion of the realm was increased in 838 by the addition of a part of Neustria.[252] *Primores* seem to refer to a somewhat indefinite group of the more important men who serve the king. It probably includes counts for it seems more than likely that counts would have been mentioned specifically as among those who commended themselves to Louis II in 877 if they had not already been included among the *primores*. The fact that vassals are mentioned with the *primores* and after them, makes it seem likely that the vassals were *not* included among the *primores* and were inferior to them in rank.[253] It is impossible to make the meaning of *primores* any more precise. *Proceres* seems to resemble *primores* in meaning. The sons of Louis II of France divided the realm inherited from their father into two parts, Louis III receiving Francia and Neustria, Caroloman receiving Burgundy and Aquitaine. Then the *proceres* commended themselves to the king in whose realm their *honores*[254] lay.[255] Just what men were included among them it is difficult to say, but the *proceres* certainly included men of important position, the principal heads of the royal administration.[256] We know definitely that Bernard, puppet king of Italy, was one of the *proceres* of Louis the Pious, and the same text informs us that *proceres* are men in service.[257] Einhard says that two *proceres* died in battle; they were both dukes, Eric of Friuli and Gerald of Bavaria.[258] Another designation for these important people who serve the king is *optimates*.[259] Hadrian II wrote one letter to the archbishops and bishops of France and a similar one to all the *optimates* of the realm; in both letters he speaks of the king as their seignior. In general, these *primores, proceres, optimates* are the chief potentates of the realm, the men who frequent the *palatium* of the king,[260] and who are wise enough or influential enough or useful enough so that the king consults them on very important matters, such as a division of the realm among his sons.[261]

Persons who served the king but in a less conventional capacity likewise commended themselves. At least two royal nephews commended themselves to the king. Bernard of Italy commended himself to his uncle Louis the Pious and swore an oath of fidelity.[262] Charles the Bald received his nephew Pepin into his commendation, obtaining also an oath of fidelity, and gave him the lordship over Aquitaine on condition that he would always be ready to bring his uncle aid in case of need.[263] Loyalty and subjection were elements in the concept of service expressed in commendation. Furthermore this was an honorable subjection.[264] Hence an act of commendation was well suited to be the form by which foreign or semi-independent princes might indicate their acceptance of Carolingian superiority. Zatun, prefect of Barcelona, commended himself to Charlemagne in 797.[265] The same king took into his commendation another Spanish prince, Abd-Allah, son of the late emir of Cordova, Abd-er-Rahman, and an exile from his own land.[266] Charles the Bald was forced by circumstances to let Respogius, son of Nomenoë, duke of Brittany, retain what was virtually a separate kingdom; [267] but Respogius at least went through the ceremony of commendation.[268] We have already seen that Salomon, duke of Brittany, commended himself to Charles the Bald in 863.[269] Harold, exiled king of the Danes, commended himself into the hands of Louis the Pious,[270] thus entering his service and becoming his *fidelis*.[271] We know that fifty years later a Danish duke named Welandus commended himself to Charles the Bald, and swore oaths along with those who were in his following.[272] In the course of a military expedition in Saxon territory in 789, Charlemagne encountered some Slavic kings who sued for peace, placed their lands under his domination, gave hostages, and apparently commended themselves to him.[273] In 884 Brazelavo, duke of the region between the Drave and the Save, placed himself in the service of Charles the Fat.[274] In the same year Zwentibaldus, duke of the Moravians, became the man of, that is, commended himself into the hands of, Charles the Fat.[275] Finally, the dukes of the Bohemians came to Arnulf and, honorably received by him into his hands in the customary fashion (i. e., commendation), they were reconciled to subordination to the royal power.[276]

It will be remembered that the exact status of the Carolingian bishops with reference to the king has been a highly controversial matter.[277] Accordingly a more de-

FIDELES 63

tailed study of their relationship to the king seems desirable. If our interpretation of *fideles* is correct, we should expect to find even the bishops commending themselves to the king as their seignior since, as we have seen, the bishops are included among the *fideles*. Again the texts substantiate our theory. In 837 when Louis the Pious established a kingdom for his son Charles, the bishops were among those who commended themselves to him and who promised fidelity on oath. There is nothing to indicate that their actions on this occasion varied in any way from that of the abbots, counts, and vassals.[278] Louis the Pious saw to it that Aldricus, bishop of Le Mans, commended himself into the hands of Charles.[279] In 869 Charles the Bald occupied Lorraine and received the bishops of Verdun, Metz, Toul, and Liége, into his commendation.[280] In 877 his son Louis II received the commentation of the bishops and the abbots, *primores* of the realm, and the vassals; the bishops, however, made a *professio* rather than an oath of fidelity, whereas the abbots, counts, and vassals promised fidelity in the customary manner, i. e., on oath.[281] In 882 the bishops commended themselves to Carloman of France.[282] Adalgarius, archbishop of Hamburg, became the king's man, that is, he commended himself to the king.[283] In 858 Louis the German invaded the realm of Charles the Bald, and scored a temporary success. The chief personage to betray Charles and to go over to Louis had been Wenilo, archbishop of Sens. With the withdrawal of Louis from the venture, Wenilo was left to face the storm. He was tried in a council, and Charles personally presented his charges against him. Among other things, the king asserted that Wenilo had been of the opinion that the bishops should put themselves under the power and in the service of

Louis, those very bishops who were pledged to Charles with a promise of faith (*fides*)[284] and who should give him the aid and counsel which they had pledged with their own hand (i. e., by commendation).[285]

Clerics other than bishops also commended themselves to the king. Charles the Bald reminded Wenilo that before he was a bishop he had commended himself to him and promised fidelity on oath in the fashion customary for clerics serving in the royal chapel.[286] In the same charges against Wenilo, we learn that Tortoldus, appointed to the see of Bayeux by Louis during his temporary occupation of part of the west Frankish kingdom, had been a cleric in Charles' commendation.[287] Clerics might commend themselves to seigniors other than the king; Jacob and Simon, priests, commended themselves into the hands of Hitto, bishop of Freising, and received a benefice.[288]

Bishops, *fideles* who have commended themselves to the king, speak of him not only as king (*rex* or *dominus rex*), but also as their seignior (*senior*). Hodingus, a priest probably already in the king's commendation, for he is called "his" priest in the *palatium*, was given the bishopric of Le Mans; the *Actus Pontificum* speaks of Charlemagne as his seignior.[289] Arno, archbishop of Salzburg, in a letter to the bishops of his province, referred to Charlemagne as the "lord our seignior."[290] The bishops in a council of 813 refer to clerics in the service of our lord (*dominus*);[291] this is probably a use of *dominus* in the narrow sense of a seignior. Aldricus, bishop of Le Mans, whom we have seen commending himself to Charles the Bald at the command of Louis the Pious,[292] spoke of his old master as the "lord Louis our seignior and most pious emperor."[293] We learn from the *Gesta Aldrici* that he adhered faithfully to his seignior Charles, and did not

FIDELES 65

desert his seignior, but remained steadfastly faithful to him and helped him with all his powers, and on his account set all things aside and followed him in all his fortunes.[294] For Anscharius, archbishop of Hamburg, Louis the German is "the most merciful lord and our seignior, King Louis."[295] At a joint meeting in 853 between Charles the Bald and Louis the German the *Capitulare Missorum Silvancense* was issued; in it the *missi* refer to the kings as "our seigniors."[296] At the end of the capitulary is a list of the *missi* sent into various districts of the western kingdom. Among them are the archbishops of Rheims, Rouen, and Sens, and the bishops of Laon, Noyon, Térouanne, Beauvais, Amiens, Lisieux, Angers, Chartres, Langres, and Autun.[297] For them the king is also their seignior. In 866 when Hermintrude, wife of Charles the Bald, became queen, two bishops in addressing their colleagues spoke of Charles as "our lord and seignior Charles, glorious king."[298] The bishops of the middle kingdom wrote to Pope Nicholas concerning the divorce of their "seignior, lord Lothair."[299] Adventius of Metz in a letter to the same pope on the same subject refers frequently to his "seignior Lothair."[300] The same bishops exercised themselves on behalf of their seignior and king in 867 when they wrote to the bishops of the realm of Charles the Bald. They had heard that some traitors within the realm of Lothair had urged Charles to attempt the seizure of his nephew's realm, encouraging him in this venture by saying that the Lorraine bishops wished Lothair expelled. "Indeed, we confess," they wrote, "that we are and wish to be faithful to our king to whom we promised steadfast fidelity when we received him as king from the hands of his father. Furthermore we cannot break the obligations of good faith and Christian oath towards our seignior and king without paying the penalty of eternal torments."[301] Following the death of Lothair, the bishops of Metz, Toul, Verdun, and Liége accepted Charles as their seignior, for they commended themselves to him.[302]

The popes recognized that the Frankish bishops had seigniors. Hadrian II in writing to the archbishops and bishops of the realm of Charles the Bald referred to the latter as their seignior.[303] John VIII addressed a letter to the bishops who had deserted Charles the Bald in 876. While their seignior Charles was in Rome receiving the imperial crown, Louis the German had invaded the western kingdom, and these traitorous bishops had joined with him in arms against their own master (*dominus*), race, and people.[304]

This commendation of the bishops to the king is no meaningless ceremony; the bishops recognize the burden of service which rests upon them in their promises of fidelity. In this respect they do not differ from lay faithful servants. In February, 876, Charles the Bald held a *placitum* at Pavia with all the bishops, abbots, counts, and other *optimates* of the Italian realm who had gathered there.[305] These unanimously chose Charles, already declared emperor,[306] as their protector, lord (*dominus*), defender, and king.[307] They then swore that they would be as faithful and obedient and helpful to their seignior as they knew how or could be, with aid and counsel in accordance with their function in all things.[308] Among those who recognized Charles as their seignior there were one archbishop, seventeen bishops, one abbot, one duke, and ten counts.[309] In a similar meeting at Pavia in 899 the bishops accepted Guy of Spoleto as their king and seignior and defender to whom they would be obedient and helpful insofar as they could.[310] After his *placitum* at Pavia

Charles the Bald returned to France and in June, 876, held a great council in which bishops from Francia, Burgundy, Aquitaine, Septimania, Neustria, and Provence confirmed his new dignities.[311] The members attending the council then promised the same oath to their seignior [312] which the bishops and *optimates* of Italy had promised at Pavia.[313] The list of those who were present and who consented and subscribed their names [314] shows that besides the papal legates, John of Toscanella and John of Arezzo,[315] seven archbishops, thirty-eight bishops, and five abbots swore fidelity to their seignior. As we have seen above,[316] the bishops commended themselves to Louis II, son of Charles the Bald, at his accession in 877, and they promised to be faithful and helpful to their seignior and king, just as a bishop should be to his seignior.[317] Hincmar, bishop of Laon, in one of his more repentant moods [318] wrote to the bishops assembled at Pitres in 868 that he would humbly give satisfaction for his misdeeds to Charles the Bald just as he ought to do to his lord and seignior and king.[319] And in 870 at the council of Attigny in the presence of his colleagues he promised to be "faithful and obedient to the lord his seignior, Charles the king, in accordance with his function just as a man (*homo*) ought to be to his seignior and as a bishop ought rightly to be to his king." [320] Hincmar, archbishop of Rheims, included himself among the *fideles* [321] of his seignior the king.[322] In a letter to Gerard, count of Vienne, in 861, Hincmar referred to Charles the Bald as his seignior.[323] During the notorious *affaire Hincmar de Laon*, the archbishop of Rheims wrote to Odo, bishop of Beauvais, a letter which has been reported by Flodoard. The writer protested that he intervened in this matter not so much on behalf of his nephew (Hincmar of Laon) as on behalf of the king his seignior to prevent the latter's committing a sin which might cause his eternal damnation.[324] According to Flodoard, Hincmar of Rheims did so much on behalf of his nephew that on his own testimony he incurred the displeasure of his seignior, the king.[325]

To conclude, the bishops of Frankland commended themselves and swore an oath or professed a promise of fidelity to the king; and they served him as their seignior. Consequently, they were numbered among the faithful servants (*fideles*) who entered service by commendation with the hands.

The evidence here presented shows that men who commend themselves for service to a seignior may be called *homines* or *fideles*. *Homines* is used more commonly for men who serve private seigniors although *fideles* can be used for such persons.[326] Men who serve the king are on the contrary more commonly called *fideles* although they are sometimes called *homines*.[327] Among these faithful servants of the king we find all the regular members of the administrative hierarchy such as bishops, abbots, dukes, counts, vassals, and other officials as well as various princes who admit their subservience to the king; all of these men appear among the ranks of the *fideles* and commend themselves to the king as their seignior.[328]

CHAPTER IV

CONCLUSION

WE MAY now proceed to a summary of our findings. There are some men in the kingdom to whom the Carolingian king gives his special protection and favor and upon whom he relies for assistance in his domestic and political affairs; these have all been called his "vassals" by many historians but this term is clearly not applicable to the whole group in the Carolingian period. They may better be called *fideles*, a term which has a narrow meaning equivalent to "faithful servants." They could also be called *homines*; the wide variety of usages for this latter term, however, coupled with its greater rarity when applied to the faithful servants of the king suggests that modern historians should be encouraged to use the term *fideles*. These *fideles* enter the service of the king by the ceremony of commending themselves into his hands. The bond which attaches them to the king is closer than that between ordinary subjects and the king, for it involves on their part an obligation not only to be loyal and obedient, but also to be helpful in ways which are possible to them because of their greater material resources. This difference between the faithful servants and the ordinary subjects which is based upon the possibility of greater usefulness finds overt expression in the words of the oath of fidelity which they usually swear at the time when they commend themselves. For the faithful servants of the king, the latter is both their king (*rex*) and seignior (*senior*) whom they serve.

The same pressures which led some men to enter the

protection and service of the king led others to enter the protection and service of various magnates who may be called private seigniors. We have fewer sources from the Carolingian period describing arrangements between these parties, but there is no reason to believe on the basis of what does exist that different methods were employed in this social nexus. The faithful servants who follow private seigniors are more commonly called *homines* than *fideles* though the latter term was used; these are general terms which may cover lay as well as clerical servants. Like the king's servants they commend themselves to their seigniors and apparently promise an oath of fidelity to their seigniors.

The faithful servants of the king who are as a group generally called *fideles* may be separated into subdivisions, the principal ones being the bishops, abbots, counts, and vassals. These are all *commendati* [329] of their seignior but they are distinguished one from another because of the differing functions which they perform. The members of each of these groups may do some things in common; they may all serve at times as *missi*. But they perform enough tasks differing one from another to mark each group off one from another. The bishop is essentially an administrator for the king of a bishopric, as the abbot is of a monastery; each must aid the king with the resources, spiritual and material, of the office with which he has been entrusted, and on occasion, with his advice and personal help. Similarly, the count is a functionary charged with administering a portion of the realm, the county, in the king's name and for the king's benefit. The vassal's function is essentially to hold himself in readiness as a completely equipped man of arms who can go wherever the king wills and stay as long as is necessary, to act as a

CONCLUSION

bodyguard, to aid the king in policing the realm, in manning garrisons, and in serving with all his equipment in the army.[330] The vassal differs from the others in that at this period he might serve a private person, though this person was generally of considerable importance and position. Although all these functionaries are *commendati*, they are not all of equal rank; the position of some is of greater dignity and honor than that of others. The bishops precede the counts and abbots, who in turn precede the vassals. But this is not to say that the position of a vassal is without honor. Quite the contrary; the vassals are among the élite of the Frankish kingdom, even if they are not of the rank of a bishop, and even though vassalage may be beneath the dignity of a prince.

It must be admitted, however, that there are a few texts which *may* be interpreted in such a way as to indicate that some men used the term *vassi* loosely, perhaps as a synonym of *fideles*, men who served the king as functionaries and were his *commendati*. If so, this use is so rare and so uncertain as to be of negligible importance *in the Carolingian period*. There is no evidence of any sort that the kings thought of imposing or attempted to impose *vassalage* upon their various functionaries.[331] So far as the king was concerned, vassals were a particular group of faithful servants entrusted with a certain function, not all persons who were in his commendation.

The interpretation of vassalage here presented does not envisage the sudden appearance of a new institution; it does not postulate an abrupt shift in the political customs of the times, there is no "explosion" of vassalage, but a steady continuity with the past. Free *vassi* cannot be followed back of the eighth century, but that does not mean that there were in earlier times no men who correspond to the *vassi* of our period. We are forced to rely for our Merovingian sources almost exclusively upon ecclesiastical literary writers who, however bad their grammar might be, harked back in vocabulary at least to earlier times. Such writers frequently seek to avoid words of vulgar origin which may be the common coin of the spoken language. *Vassus* was such a word. Though in the capitularies *vassi* appears without apology, the writer of the *Vita Hludowici Imperatoris* felt constrained to explain when he employed it that it was a word in common use.[332] As late as 870 Hincmar of Rheims gave evidence of a similar awkward feeling in using this word.[333] We need not be surprised then if *vassus* did not appear in the earlier literary sources. But the thing was not lacking, even if the word was. The Merovingian sources are full of *pueri, viri fortissimi, milites, satellites, custodes, amici, gasindi*, who are nothing but professional soldiers, military retainers of kings, queens, bishops, and royal functionaries, and other rich men, as has been well shown by Guilhiermoz.[334] They are the predecessors under another name of the Carolingian *vassi*.[335] What is perhaps new in Carolingian vassalage is the attempt made by the king to regularize it in law and to control it, but even here we cannot be too sure because of the paucity of the sources.

As for Carolingian commendation, its continuity with the past is unbroken. As far back as the days of the republic in Rome, the humble client fastened himself to his patron by commendation; in return for protection and the *sportula*, he voted for his patron and followed him in his public life. By the time of Diocletian and his successors, the great men of the empire, the great functionaries of state, were among the imperial clients. Whether this commendation of Roman days was accompanied by the touch-

CONCLUSION 73

ing of hands we do not know, for the texts do not describe the ceremony of commendation. The obligation of the client towards his patron was not yet military.[336] Under the Merovingians commendation continued apace, and perhaps the hand played a part in the ceremony. Counts, dukes, and bishops, as well as humbler men, commended themselves into service just as their successors did under the Carolingians. The *commendati* owed *servitium et obsequium*.[337] The king had in his commendation men who served him as soldiers, and magnates were surrounded by armed men who served them.[338] The continuity then between the pre-Carolingian and Carolingian periods is not in the least broken by this interpretation of vassalage. Of course, with the dissolution of the Carolingian empire, commendation began to play a rôle of paramount importance denied it in earlier times. There is no need to discuss here its importance for subsequent European development.

The explanation of vassalage which has been presented in these pages does not revolutionize our understanding of the Carolingian period, nor upset any of the main doctrines which have been held by historians concerning this period. It does not demand a new delineation of the main lines of Carolingian political life and institutions. On the contrary, it indicates a more appropriate name, *fidelis*, for a familiar friend, the *commendatus*. It reveals clearly the status of the bishops. Furthermore, it clarifies previous notions about Carolingian vassalage and makes them more consistent with the texts; for it helps to unravel certain ambiguities which have resulted from the two contradictory tendencies indicated in the introduction. On the one hand, it does not deny the inclusion of the *vassi* among the *commendati*, the fact which inspired some historians to identify vassalage and commendation. On the other hand, it justifies the misgivings of others who felt that certain of these men who commended themselves into service were not quite "real" vassals. Furthermore, the characterization of vassals here presented does not alter most of our understanding of vassalage, that is, the description of "real" vassals. Thus, what this interpretation has taken with one hand, it has largely handed back with the other in an improved form.

APPENDIX I

COMMENDATION AND THE OATH OF FIDELITY

AT LEAST as early as the year 757 [339] it became the practice for magnates who commended themselves to the king to accompany this ceremony with an oath of fidelity.[340] A typical case is to be found in connection with the establishment in 837 of an appanage realm for Charles the Bald; the bishops, abbots, counts, and *vassalli dominici* who held benefices in the realm assigned to Charles commended themselves to him with an oath (*se commendaverunt et fidelitatem iuramento firmaverunt*).[341] The oath which was sworn on such occasions reflected the status of the swearers and accordingly differed from the oath sworn by the mass of subjects. The Carolingian rulers asked their subjects to swear that they would be faithful without deceit or illwill; their oath was essentially a promise to be obedient and to refrain from disloyalty. The magnates, on the other hand, who were servants of the king, swore that they would be faithful helpers with aid and counsel; thus their oath was not a promise of mere loyalty, for it entailed an obligation of positive service.[342]

The question has frequently been raised: Which of these two ceremonies, commendation (homage) or the oath of fidelity, was the essential one in establishing the service relationship, in creating the bond of "vassalage" between a man and his seignior? Flach,[343] Esmein,[344] and Lot [345] have favored the oath of fidelity at the expense of commendation or homage. The fullest presentation of this view is that by Dumas, who says that it is the oath of fidelity which is essential; homage is only an accessory formality.[346] Fidelity, not homage, is the basis of the relationship of "vassalage." Homage is only an empty form which implies, to be sure, a certain subordination of one person to another but which indicates by itself no precise obligations. Homage is only a mold into which one can pour all kinds of contracts. To determine its content, it must be accompanied by a special promise. Thus the homage of a "vassal" to his seignior is followed by an oath of fidelity, coming after homage, which determines the consequences. By itself, homage incurs no obligations; the duties of a "vassal" toward his seignior flow from the oath of fidelity and not from the homage.[347]

Homage likewise has its champions. Guilhiermoz presented Dumas' position in reverse; for him, fidelity is the empty form, a general defensive alliance lacking precise character. It is homage which identifies and limits the obligations incurred by fidelity.[348] Petot says that the entrance into service was effected by commendation.[349] If royal servants who had commended themselves followed their homage with the swearing of an oath of fidelity, they did so as ordinary subjects, swearing the oath of ordinary subjects; this oath has nothing to do with their obligations as "vassals."[350] Indeed, their commendation is not to be confused with the oath of fidelity; commendation is not an empty form, the content of which must be indicated by an oath of fidelity.[351] Bloch is in agreement with Petot; homage is the real creator of the service relationship in its double aspect of dependence and protection. When the two rites are joined, the pre-eminence of homage is indicated by its coming first in the ceremony. The swearing of an oath of fidelity is a banal affair which may be repeated a number of times; homage is a more serious business. There are many acts of fidelity without homages, but there are no homages without acts of fidelity.[352]

Thus, the "essential" element in creating the service relationship is for some the oath of fidelity whereas for others it is homage. Waitz, however, said that the service relationship, "vassalage" as he called it, depended always upon the combination of the two elements; the distinguishing feature of this relationship is in fact the union of the two.[353] He held to this formulation despite the difficulty he incurred in dealing with the bishops. Though they commended themselves and promised fidelity and so effected this union, Waitz still shrank from calling this instance "vassalage."[354] This curious inconsistency was, of course, one of his own making, the result of his calling "vassalage" this relationship of service established by commendation and fidelity.

What does seem to be a proper description of the relationship of commendation to the oath of fidelity? It should be noted first that the two acts are separate and distinct ceremonies even though they are joined together.[355] The texts separate them (*se commendare et fidelitatem iurare*)[356] and a few commendations are mentioned without references being made to oaths of fidelity.[357] The hero of a battle against the Saracens, a certain John, received as a reward for his services the manor of Fontes; the charter which informs us of his exploit says that John commended himself into Charlemagne's hands and then, *fidelis noster*, asked for the concession of the manor; no mention is made in the charter of an oath of fidelity.[358] A capitulary of Lothair I is addressed to those who have commended themselves to him; these are magnates for he speaks of the free men who are in their commendation; there is no word of fidelity.[359] The *Gesta Aldrici* says only that Aldricus commended himself *per manus* to Charles the Bald.[360] At the time when Charles the Bald acquired Lorraine, only the commendation of the bishops of Metz, Toul, Verdun, and Liége is mentioned.[361] When Adalgarius, successor of Rimbert, bishop of Hamburg (865–888), still in the lifetime of Rimbert became the *homo* of the king *per manus*, he may have sworn an oath of fidelity, but nothing is said about it in the texts.[362] When Louis III and Carloman after the death of their father divided his realm between them in 880, the *proceres* commended themselves to the young kings; again, no oath of fidelity is mentioned.[363] The fact that in these cases nothing is said about the swearing of an oath does not mean necessarily that no such oath was sworn. It does indicate, however, that commendation was a ceremony separate from the oath of fidelity. This ceremony might be, and usually was, accompanied by the oath of fidelity.[364]

The essential thing in the establishment of the service relationship was the agreement between the two men concerned to enter such a relationship. Commendation and the oath of fidelity were only the outward and visible signs of such an agreement. Homage was an impressive ceremony by which the man placed himself before the eyes of the world in the hands of his seignior; this act was what might be termed a "secular" pledge of service. It was inevitable that in a religious world there would be joined to this a ceremony involving a religious sanction to guarantee the fulfilment of the bargain entered into by the two parties.³⁶⁵ The man promised on sacred relics to be a faithful helper with aid and counsel, and hence if he broke his pledge to his seignior, he would feel the dreadful vengeance of the enraged saints and God. The same obligation is incurred in each act.³⁶⁶ Thus, the man who has commended himself and sworn fidelity to his seignior is pledged before man and God to be a loyal helper to his seignior.

Thus the answer to the question, which is the "essential" element, homage or fidelity, is that the question should not be asked at all. As Calmette says, this question historically has no meaning.³⁶⁷ Both are the outward signs of the establishment of a service relationship, and customarily the oath followed upon homage. It is not surprising under these circumstances that those who were in the king's service were usually called his *fideles*. They were men who had sworn an oath of fidelity to him personally, and in accordance with that oath they rendered him frequent service. They were his *fideles* in a very real and practical sense.

Did men who commended themselves to private seigniors also promise an oath of fidelity to them? Unfortunately, the sources tell us less about the relations between private seigniors and their men than about those between the king and his men. There is no evidence to prove that they actually did promise an oath to a private seignior in the Merovingian period,³⁶⁸ but a text from the Carolingian period refers to an oath to a private seignior. Charlemagne ordered in 805 that oaths of fidelity were to be promised to none save to himself and to one's own seignior.³⁶⁹ Although all other texts referring to private commendation mention only the act of commendation, it does not seem too bold to interpret this text as an indication of a common practice.³⁷⁰ There are several cases of the application of the term *fideles* to men serving private seigniors. This usage may well have been encouraged by the practice of swearing an oath of fidelity to the seignior.³⁷¹

Despite its frequent association with vassalage in historical literature, the oath of fidelity is of no value in an attempt to answer the cardinal problem of this study: who are Carolingian vassals? One cannot with the oath of fidelity determine how narrow or how broad the group of vassals is. The oath of fidelity was sworn by all types who entered the king's service, by *all* his *fideles* (faithful servants). The oath in no way distinguished one group of these *fideles* from another; all types of *fideles*, bishops, abbots, dukes, counts, and royal vassals, all commended themselves and swore fidelity, so far as the sources indicate, in exactly the same way.[372]

APPENDIX II

FURTHER DIFFICULTIES CONCERNING VASSALAGE

EXAMPLES other than those given in the introductory chapter likewise reveal the difficulties which historians have encountered in attempts to interpret Carolingian vassalage. One of the chief stumbling blocks is the question of the vassalage of the great officials. Dahn's account of these matters is very confusing. On one occasion he says that the man who is to become a vassal commends himself into the hands of his future seignior who usually gives him a benefice in turn.[373] Elsewhere he questions whether the *Handreichung* is the essential ceremony of vassalage and doubts that *tradere ad procerem* means *tradere se vassallum*.[374] He adds that gradually in Carolingian times the oath of fidelity became the essential form, not for all acts of commendation, but only for that into vassalage.[375] A wide variety of people, he says, commend themselves and are called vassals: petty unfree men, dukes and archbishops, margraves, palace knights, as well as foreign princes.[376] He admits, furthermore, difficulty in distinguishing between vassalage and office; in many cases it is not clear to him whether the sources mean one or the other, or both bound in a personal union. Frequently the officials were vassals; the king gave offices to his vassals. But even when the vassals were not officials, they had similar duties, rights, and privileges. Bishops, priests, and counts are sometimes vassals, but even where bishops, abbots, and counts are not vassals, they have similar responsibilities. Nor can one assert that each official had to be a vassal.[377] Dahn admits himself that this matter is not transparently clear.[378]

Despite the fact that he mentions certain difficulties which would appear to call into question the vassalage of functionaries, Dumas sweeps them aside and continues to equate commendation with vassalage. He says that vassalage was the act by which one free man put himself at the service of another free man.[379] Originally it was the king who gathered together the largest group of vassals and who pointed the way for the magnates. These vassals were at the disposal of the prince for whatever tasks he chose to give them. One could consider them regular royal functionaries of high rank who took their place immediately after the counts.[380] Yet Dumas adds that in the ninth century all the magnates were assimilated into the group of royal vassals. He admits that it is rare for the texts to give this quality of vassalage to the dukes, counts, bishops, and abbots; and that they are usually mentioned separately. He suggests, presumably as the reason for this silence in the texts, that these men are dignitaries of a higher rank than that of the royal vassals. However, despite the fact that the texts rarely call these higher dignitaries vassals, Dumas does so because, as he says, they all performed homage followed by an oath, the ceremony which for him establishes vassalage.[381]

It is difficult to decide whether or not Lot in his more recent work on vassalage has any reservations about the vassalage of officers. He says that public service comes under the influence of vassalage. Vassalage supplants other forms of commendation. The great officials, dukes, counts, marquises, bishops, and abbots perform homage like *simples vassaux*.[382] What does he mean by this statement? Who are the *simples vassaux*? What is the relationship of bishops, abbots, and counts to them? Are the simple vassals the *vassi dominici*? It seems likely, for Lot says that the Carolingians wished their *vassi dominici* to be respected equally with counts, bishops, and abbots.[383] Lot says also that the sons and nephews of the king were considered as his vassals.[384] Are they his vassals, or are they only considered as in some sense vassals?

Bloch states clearly the belief that the officials were vassals despite the fact that his description of vassalage is such as to make the rôle inappropriate for them. He describes vassals as military men attached to great households.[385] These vassals were recruited from among the upper classes, from men who were accustomed above all to fighting and to giving commands.[386] Having thus suffused vassalage with a martial light, Bloch then proceeds to say that the Carolingians used vassalage to reinforce the weakening fidelity of their functionaries. More and more frequently, these functionaries were recruited from among the king's vassals. Beginning at least with the reign of

Louis the Pious there were no holders of court posts or important commands, no counts, who had not made themselves by commendation with their hands the king's vassals. As early as the mid-eighth century foreign princes who recognized the Frankish protectorate became the king's vassals. But what does this have to do with the military vassalage he has described? Bloch adds that, of course, none of these great magnates actually mounted guard in the dwelling of their master. Yet, in their way they belonged to the military establishment, for they owed above all military help. These magnates in turn extended the ties of vassalage to their companions and helpers. In this connection Bloch refers to the bishops and abbots as well as the counts.[387] Are these prelates also vassals? He repeats again the statement that the Carolingians attached by the bonds of vassalage those to whom they entrusted the great territorial offices, especially the counties, marches, and duchies.[388] One may perhaps still be permitted to wonder about the relationship between military vassalage and officeholding.

A similar question arises on reading the work of Brunner. He describes at length the military activity of vassals.[389] He also remarks that the Carolingians filled the higher offices with their vassals and encouraged or permitted the entrance of the higher officials into vassalage.[390] He does not discuss the compatibility of military vassalage with that of the functionaries. Stephenson's remarks call to mind the same query.[391]

Another difficulty which we have noted is that with regard to the status of the bishops. Brunner speaks of an attempt made by them to avoid "commendation with an oath of fidelity," the ceremonies which establish vassalage, according to him.[392] Dopsch goes farther and gives to the clergy a special status. He says in orthodox fashion that the vassal relationship was established in Frankish times by commendation[393] and that vassals are "persons who have entered commendation."[394] He does not discuss directly the question whether or not bishops, abbots, and counts were vassals. It is evident, however, from one passage that he does not regard clerics and women as vassals, but rather as persons "obligated to give fidelity and service."[395] Their commendation somehow does not entail vassalage.

APPENDIX II 83

Lesne reveals the same inclination to grant the bishops a special status within vassalage, so to speak. He says that the bishops are faithful servants (*fidèles*) placed by the king side by side with abbots, counts, and other *fidèles*. Like all the others, bishops promise fidelity and commend themselves.[396] It seems, furthermore, that bishops and abbots as well as counts are not only *fidèles* but also in a sense vassals. For Lesne says that when the capitularies and annals enumerate the different categories of royal vassals, the prelates appear with the counts and other vassals. Could the person of the bishop or abbot be spared from the rising tide of vassal ideas and institutions of the time? No, says Lesne; the new bonds which attach the churches to the crown and the prelates to the king subject the prelates to responsibilities and duties unknown in earlier times.[397] The prelates, one infers, do become vassals. The same conclusion seems to follow from other remarks. The counts and other *hommes du roi*, he says had to give the king gifts. Prelates were held to this like other *fidèles*. Bishops and abbots paid the *annua dona* of vassals. If the prelates were held for this regular contribution, it was because of the development of vassalage, which created new obligations for them toward the king, their *senior*.[398] Despite these statements, Lesne says that the bishops were not considered the king's vassals even though they had sworn an oath of fidelity. He explains that in these respects the words (*formes de langage*) showed deference to the habits and rules of ecclesiastical discipline in spite of the invasion by royal law of the old canon law.[399] Lesne seems to think that bishops behaved like vassals except in that they did not call themselves, and were not called, vassals out of respect for canon law.

In one particular at least the position of Ehrenberg differs from that of any other author. The general tendency is to equate vassalage with commendation, and then, if there are any misgivings, to raise the possibility that vassalage is a narrower category than commendation. According to Ehrenberg, however, a man may be a vassal without having commended himself to his seignior. To be sure, he says that to commend oneself is to become a vassal. In indicating the phrases by which an act of commendation is designated, he places side by

VASSI AND FIDELES

side as equivalents the following: "se commendare . . . in vassaticum se commendare . . . in vassatico oder in sua commendatione oder in fidem recipere . . . vassus (vassallus) fieri." [400] But vassalage is broader than commendation; hence, the two should not be equated. Although he who commends himself to another becomes a vassal, not everyone who is a vassal has commended himself to his lord. This follows from the fact that there are unfree men who have been made vassals by their masters.[401] Ehrenberg concludes, therefore, that vassals are privileged servants, whether free or unfree.[402] Note, however, that free men who commend themselves become by that act vassals; and that Ehrenberg includes foreign princes among the vassals.[403]

APPENDIX III

THE BISHOPS' LETTER FROM KIERSY IN 858

ON SEPTEMBER 1, 858 Louis the German invaded the realm of Charles the Bald.[404] At first everything went in favor of the invader. Charles, engaged in besieging a Norman encampment, permitted Louis to march about with his army unmolested for some weeks. Magnates from Neustria, Brittany, and Aquitaine came to subject themselves to Louis. By November 12, all efforts on Charles' part to negotiate with Louis having failed, the two brothers faced each other in battle array at Brienne-le-Château. The expected battle did not take place. Some of Charles' troops deserted him; and losing confidence in the rest, he suddenly fled to Burgundy, leaving Louis apparently undisputed master of the north of France. Louis, relying on the support of the West Franks who had deserted Charles for him, allowed his German troops to return home, and began dispensing *honores* right and left to seal the newly acquired loyalty of Charles' former subjects.

Only two things seemed to be lacking to Louis: the acceptance of him by the bishops, of whom so far only one, Wenilo of Sens, had come over to him, and their consecration of him as king in the west. Relying upon the authority of success, Louis summoned the bishops to a council to be held at Rheims on November 25, announcing as the purpose of the meeting that he wished to consult with them concerning the restoration of Holy Church and concerning the condition and safety of the Christian people. Instead of obeying this summons, the bishops of the provinces of Rheims and Rouen gathered at Kiersy outside the reach of Louis at the moment, and from there they sent to him at Attigny a letter which was a masterpiece of diplomacy.[405] It came from the able pen of Hincmar of Rheims as he himself admitted.[406]

In that letter is the following passage: "Et nos episcopi Domino consecrati non sumus huiusmodi homines, ut, sicut homines saeculares, in vassallatico debeamus nos cuilibet commendare." [407]

Before translating it, let us see what situation the bishops faced at the time this was written. An invader had entered the land and had been well received by many of the magnates. The rightful king had departed to a distant part of the realm without striking a blow. Thus though the chances seemed to favor Louis, Charles still remained a possible and probable contender for the royal title. A civil war of the kind the bishops remembered only too well was a certainty if Louis remained in the west. Furthermore, the bishops' sympathies seem to have lain with Charles even though they felt that he had misgoverned the realm in some respects. Therefore, they favored the return to power of Charles. But to defy Louis openly at this moment would be dangerous and might bring about an immediate defeat of their hopes. What the bishops needed was time, time in which the fortunes of Charles might revive, time in which he might gather together an army; and that is exactly what the bishops succeeded in getting.

Louis must actually have desired an immediate pronouncement in his favor by the powerful bishops. In order to get it, he sought to entice them into his presence by proclaiming that he had come to right the wrongs committed by his brother upon a people who had called on him for help. For this work of reform he needed the assistance of the bishops. Would they come to advise him concerning the restoration of Holy Church and concerning the condition and safety of the Christian people? How could the bishops resist such a pious and righteous appeal? They would have to come.

The bishops responded but not in the way Louis had hoped. In their letter to him they appeared to accept his professions of good intentions; indeed one would hardly suspect from the tone of the letter that Louis had invaded the realm at all. They do not discuss openly the merits or demerits of his claim to the throne; they neither openly accept nor reject him. They simply excuse themselves from coming to him at present because of the shortness of the time before the date set for the council and its inconvenience, because of the inconvenience of the place set for the meeting, and because of the present disturbances; and later

APPENDIX III

in their letter they add another excuse, the approach of Christmas.[408]

If for these various reasons they cannot come in person to advise him, they send him plenty of advice by letter. They remind him at length (c. 4) that he himself must one day face the Lord's judgment, and that the Christian lands (c. 5) are afflicted by the ravages of pagans; he should attack them. They thus imply that if he loves justice and his own soul, he might better be attacking the enemies of God rather than his own brother. Then (c. 7) they give him a great deal of advice on how a good ruler should act, how he should protect his subjects and the Church and ecclesiastical foundations. He should rule (c. 12) so that he renders to God the things that are God's; he should constitute as his agents God-fearing men. They utter a threat against men who defy law and justice (c. 13). The king should establish (c. 14) good men as administrators of the royal villas. Most of this advice was for the benefit of Charles the Bald[409] rather than for Louis; nevertheless, it was what Louis had openly asked for, though hardly what he wanted.

The bishops finally came to a point which must have interested Louis much more.[410] As if to defend themselves from a possible charge of disobedience or infidelity, they say: "We ought and wish to believe you such that you would not wish to increase your realm at the cost of your soul, nor to receive us as helpers in ecclesiastical affairs and government if we were dishonored with the loss of the priesthood, as would be the case if, against God and the authority of reason, we should be zealous (*studuerimus*) in commending ourselves and our churches to you." Notice that this is not a final refusal to commend themselves and the churches. It would simply be against the will of God and unreasonable to do it with indecent haste! The bishops were walking a tightrope and doing it well. "For indeed the churches entrusted to us by God are not benefices or property of the king of a kind that he can give them away or take them away out of mere whim and without advice (*pro libitu suo inconsulte*)." They take again a middle ground; they do not deny that the king has any rights over the property of the church. "Since all things of the church are consecrated to God, whoever defrauds, or takes anything away from, the church is known to have committed a sacrilege according to the Scriptures."

The bishops have been referring to the property of the Church; now they refer to their personal position. "We bishops consecrated to God are not men of such a kind that we should commend ourselves into vassalage like secular men." In these circumstances the bishops are doing their best to emphasize their ecclesiastical responsibilities, to excuse themselves from secular responsibilities, such as attending the king or providing military aid. They do not commend themselves into vassalage; they do not serve the king in that capacity.[411] No, they commend themselves and their churches "for protecting, and helping in the government of, ecclesiastical affairs";[412] that is their job.

Furthermore, "we ought not in any way to swear an oath which evangelical and apostolic and canonical authority forbids," for the hand which, anointed with holy oil, performs the sacrament of the Eucharist should not touch any secular sacrament, nor should the tongue of the bishop which is through the grace of God the key to Heaven, swear like a secular tongue in the name of God and the saints.

The bishops are here endeavoring to avoid making what Louis wanted very much to have them make, an ordinary commendation involving the performance of secular tasks and an oath of fidelity. The issue was never fought out, for Louis' good fortune suddenly changed for the worse when the bishops failed to give him their active support. Charles came back with an army; without striking a blow, Louis fled back to Germany.

The bishops' objections [413] to the swearing of an oath were respected at Gondreville in 872 when the bishops made a *professio* whereas the lay *fideles* swore an oath.[414] When Louis II became king of France in 877 [415] the bishops commended themselves and their churches for the defense due and the canonical privileges which were assured them; in return for this protection, they too were to give service, for they professed (*profitentes*) that they would be faithful with aid and counsel in accordance with their knowledge and ability and according to their offices; the abbots, *primores* of the realm, and royal vassals commended themselves to him, and promised fidelity on

APPENDIX III

oath in customary fashion. The procedure of the bishops differed in that they *professed* what the others *promised on oath*. The actual formulae have the same elements as the oath of the *fideles* in 858, fidelity plus aid and counsel according to their office.

Waitz regarded the statement of 858 as an attempt on the part of the bishops to escape from the loyalty which characterized a vassal,[416] a danger into which he felt that they were falling, because he regarded vassalage as the union of an act of commendation with an oath of fidelity.[417] Brunner and Dahn were of the same opinion.[418]

Imbart de la Tour saw in this statement an attempt made by the bishops to turn commendation into a request for protection without the element of service in return, an attempt which was not acknowledged by the state.[419] But even this attempt seems to have been inspired by the special circumstances of the case; for as Lesne has pointed out, Hincmar of Rheims may have attempted to free the bishops of secular responsibilities at a time when they would have been called upon to work against their rightful king; at a later date, however, he showed remarkable complaisance when the bishops of Lorraine commended themselves to Charles the Bald.[420]

In conclusion, there is no reason to infer that the bishops had found themselves caught in *vassalage* and that in 858 they made an effort to escape from its meshes. On the other hand, in the face of very unusual circumstances [421] they made an effort to escape the secular service which was just as much a part of commendation as the royal protection given in return for it. They called attention to the fact that they, consecrated to God, were not men of such a kind that they, as if they were secular men, could commend themselves to give service such as that given by vassals. A reference to military service was particularly apt at this time. They knew perfectly well that Louis wanted their military assistance, and to avoid giving it they planned an excuse beforehand. Once the invader had left the realm, the matter was dropped, and the bishops made no further effort in this period to transform the nature of commendation so as to avoid serving the king.[422]

APPENDIX IV

KRAWINKEL'S INTERPRETATION OF THE TASSILO CASE

HERMANN KRAWINKEL has discussed at some length the tangled affairs of Tassilo.[423] Krawinkel asserts that Tassilo could not have commended himself into vassalage at Compiègne in 757 and that accordingly the accounts given by the court annals, the *Annales Regni Francorum* and the *Annales Einhardi*, are later falsifications to establish precedents for the actions of Charlemagne in 787 which led to the downfall of the rebellious Tassilo in 788. He calls attention [424] to the fact that at the very same council held at Compiègne where Tassilo "supposedly" commended himself into vassalage a decree was issued concerning the marital difficulties of an *unfree* vassal. Could this unfree vassal be a "colleague" of Tassilo? Could the term "vassal" be applied at the very same time to the duke of Bavaria? Surely not, says Krawinkel. The court annalists must have falsified the political events of 757. Hence Krawinkel proceeds to look for evidence to substantiate this belief.

He makes much of minor variations for the events of 757 in the *Annales Regni Francorum* and its somewhat later version, the *Annales Einhardi*. Let us see the texts: [425]

Annales Regni Francorum (the older version): ". . . Pippinus tenuit placitum suum in Compendio cum Francis; ibique Tassilo venit, dux Baioariorum, in vassatico se commendans per manus, sacramenta iuravit multa et innumerabilia, reliquias sanctorum manus inponens, et fidelitatem promisit regi Pippino et supradictis filiis eius, domno Carolo et Carlomanno, sicut vassus recta mente et firma devotione per iustitiam, sicut vassus dominos suos esse deberet. Sic confirmavit supradictus Tassilo supra corpus sancti Dionisii, Rustici et Eleutherii necnon et sancti Germani seu sancti Martini, ut omnibus diebus vitae eius sic conservaret, sicut sacramentis promiserat; sic et eius homines maiores natu, qui erant cum eo, firmaverunt, sicut dictum est, in locis superius nominatis quam et in aliis multis."

Annales Einhardi (the new version): ". . . in Conpendio . . . ubi tunc populi sui generalem conventum habuit. Illuc et Tassilo dux

APPENDIX IV 91

Baioariorum cum primoribus gentis suae venit et more Francico in manus regis in vassaticum manibus suis semetipsum commendavit fidelitatemque tam ipso regi Pippino quam filiis eius Karlo et Carlomanno iureiurando supra corpus sancti Dionysii promisit; et non solum ibi, sed etiam super corpus sancti Martini et sancti Germani simili sacramento fidem se praedictis dominis suis diebus vitae suae servaturum est pollicitus. Similiter et omnes primores ac maiores natu Baioarii, qui cum eo in praesentiam regis pervenerant, fidem se regi et filiis eius servaturos in praedictis venerabilibus locis promiserunt."'

There is no disputing the unusually specific description of this affair in both annals, a fact which may very well be explained by its unusual character. Krawinkel detects,[426] however, an overstressing, an element of exaggeration, in the older version. It stresses the confirmation of the ceremony with phrases using *sic confirmavit, sic conservaret, sicut promiserat, sic et eius homines . . . firmaverunt, sicut dictum est*. What does the new version say? Krawinkel does not single the phrases out but they mean the same thing. The *sic confirmavit* phrase corresponds to the newer *super corpus sancti Martini et sancti Germani simili sacramento*; the *sic conservaret* to the *fidem se . . . servaturum*; and the *sicut promiserat* to the *est pollicitus*. He says that the older version makes the Bavarian nobles commend themselves into vassalage whereas in the newer version there is the more indefinite phrase *similiter . . . fidem promiserunt*. But the older version says nothing of the kind; it says only that they confirmed what took place (*eius homines maiores natu . . . firmaverunt*). If either phrase is stronger, it is the newer one. In the older version oaths are sworn on the relics of St. Denis, St. Germanus, St. Martin, St. Rusticus, and St. Eleutherius; in the newer version this list of saints is reduced to a more "credible" number, says Krawinkel, by the exclusion of St. Rusticus and St. Eleutherius. Why does this seem more credible? The older version adds two other elements lacking in the newer: two *sicut vassus* phrases and a reference to oaths sworn in many other places (*in aliis multis*). From these differences, real or imagined, Krawinkel concludes that the older version gives evidence of over-emphasis as compared with the newer "improved" version. Granted that these variations represent an attempt to "improve" the story, why were these changes made in the newer version? Between the time of writing of the two versions lies the pardon of Charlemagne and the formal renunciation of pretensions to Bavaria by Tassilo in 794. The second "improved" version thus shows a "weakening" or softening.

Having set up this case, Krawinkel proceeds to undermine it himself by saying that the newer version not only weakens the older account, in one particular it strengthens it. It adds that Tassilo commended himself *more Francico*. Furthermore, where the older account reads *homines maiores natu qui erant cum eo*, the newer reads *et omnes primores ac maiores natu Baioarii qui cum eo in praesentiam regis pervenerant*. Then, to quote Krawinkel,[427] "die Änderung erscheint unbedeutend, genügt aber, um den Relativsatz doppelsinnig zu machen. Wer nur die neue Fassung liest, muss verstehen 'alle edlen Bayern kamen zum König.' Denn wer übersetzt 'alle diejenigen Bayern usw.,' vergisst, dass ihm oben mitgeteilt worden ist 'gentis suae'." Would it not have been sufficient to dismiss this variation as insignificant?

This analysis of the two versions leads Krawinkel to the conclusion [428] that there are exaggerations in the older version of the affair in 757 and variations in the account given by the later. Thus he doubts the truth of the "asserted" commendation into vassalage of Tassilo in 757. To bolster up this conclusion, so tenuously established on the basis of internal evidence in the court annals themselves, Krawinkel resorts to a liberal use of the argument *ex silentio*. He calls attention [429] to the fact that the continuator of Fredegarius had nothing to say about this commendation into vassalage in 757. The independent behavior of Tassilo towards the Carolingians in subsequent years argues likewise against a commendation into vassalage in 757.[430] There is no question about Tassilo's independent behavior later, but promises are not always recognizable in their fulfillment, and treaties are not always transferred from paper to actual politics. Tassilo has left, in fact, a heavy trail of broken promises across the Carolingian annals. In 763 Tassilo deserted the army of Pepin, returned to Bavaria and declared that he would never again look upon the face of Pepin. One

APPENDIX IV 93

would expect, says Krawinkel,[431] that the court annalists would say something about the service which a vassal owed to his lord. Instead, they "complain somewhat pathetically" that Tassilo had forgotten his promises to Pepin and the benefits he had received from Pepin. Neither annalist [432], it may be said, leaves any doubt as to the interpretation of Tassilo's conduct, as to his infidelity. According to the *Annales Regni Francorum*, "Tassilo dux Baioariorum postposuit sacramenta et omnia, quae promiserat, et per malum ingenium se inde seduxit, omnia benefacta, quae Pippinus rex avunculus eius ei fecit, postposuit; per ingenia fraudulenta se subtrahendo Baioariam petiit et nusquam amplius faciem supradicti regis videre voluit." According to the *Annales Einhardi*, "de qua expeditione Tassilo Baioariae dux aegritudine per dolum simulata patriam reversus est firmatoque ad defectionem animo ad regis conspectum ulterius se venturum abiuravit." The silence with regard to vassalage of these entries for 763 argues, according to Krawinkel, that Tassilo was not at that date a vassal. But Krawinkel pushes these texts too hard. If the annalists had gone out of their way to fabricate out of whole cloth the vassalage of 757, one would expect them to insert at each opportunity a reminder of that vassalage rather than to shrink from mentioning it subsequently. On the other hand, granting the validity of the earlier vassalage of Tassilo, the remarks of the annalists indicate clearly that Tassilo's conduct was certainly not in line with obligations which he would have as a vassal.

Once again, says Krawinkel,[433] these same forgers forget to remember the responsibilities of vassalage which supposedly rested upon Tassilo. In 781 Tassilo swore before Charlemagne that he would keep the promises which he had earlier made to Pepin, that he would be subservient and obedient (*subiectus et obediens*, according to the *Annales Einhardi*). This time there is no mention of vassalage. But that is not surprising in view of the circumstances of this meeting. To establish peace between Tassilo and Charlemagne, the pope had sent two legates; and Charlemagne had sent two *missi* to arrange a meeting. *After receiving hostages from Charlemagne*, Tassilo presented himself before the king to renew his oaths. If Charlemagne had to secure the arbitral help of the papacy and had to give hostages to Tassilo to persuade the latter to come to this meeting, he was hardly in a position at this time to impose the humiliating term "vassal" upon Tassilo.

Having thus exhausted the argument *ex silentio*, Krawinkel then proceeds to speculate on the possibility of an alliance between Bavaria and Aquitaine, which however true it might be, has no bearing on the question whether or not Tassilo entered by commendation into vassalage in 757.

As for the commendation into vassalage forced upon Tassilo in 787, Krawinkel accepts it [434] as a fact without hesitation. He admits [435] that the best reason for doubting the vassalage of 757 is a "terminological" one, the ascription of vassalage at the same time to Tassilo as well as to an unfree man. The same reason, however, would cast doubt upon the vassalage of 787 for still at that date the term "vassal" could be applied to an unfree man; a capitulary of 786 or 792, thus closely contemporary with 787, refers to *servi* who have been honored with vassalage.[436] Though this capitulary is actually mentioned by Krawinkel elsewhere,[437] it does not lead him to a scrutiny of the account for 787. The changes between the newer and the older versions which Krawinkel has indicated touching on affairs in 757, 763, and 781, are insignificant as compared with the variation in 787.[438] The older version says that Tassilo, under pressure from every side, came to Charlemagne and gave himself with his hands into the hands of the lord king Charles in vassalage; he received back the duchy which had been entrusted to him by the lord king Pepin and he admitted that he had sinned in all respects and had acted badly; he renewed his oaths and gave to the king his son Theodo and twelve other hostages, and then the king went back to Frankland. The *Annales Einhardi* on the contrary say nothing whatever about vassalage; according to them Tassilo, seeing that he was besieged on every side, came as a suppliant and begged that pardon be granted him for his earlier deeds; the king, who was very lenient by nature, spared him since he came as a suppliant and penitent; he received from Tassilo Theodo and twelve other hostages whom he demanded; with the fidelity of the people of the land assured by oaths, he returned to Frankland.[439] Are we then to assume that the writer of the *Annales Einhardi* knew nothing

APPENDIX IV 95

of an act of commendation into vassalage in 787 or suppressed a lie? I think not. In the very next year he refers to Tassilo as a "vassal"; Charlemagne called a council and ordered Tassilo the duke and his other vassals to attend (*Tassilonem ducem sicut et ceteros vassos suos in eodem conventu adesse iussisset*). This should be compared with the corresponding phrase of the earlier version (*ibique veniens Tassilo ex iussione domni regis, sicut et ceteri eius vassi*).[440] So far as both versions are concerned, Tassilo's status is the same, that of a vassal. If Tassilo's commendation into vassalage in 757 is to be set aside as a fabrication, then that of 787 can with as good or better reason be set aside.

It might be tempting to dispose of the whole question of Tassilo's vassalage by denying all validity to these famous texts. However, I do not believe that they can be dismissed so lightly. Krawinkel does not even attempt to set aside the vassalage of 787, and there is even less reason to set aside the vassalage of 757. Are there grounds to rule out either of these events as fabrications? I can see no trustworthy evidence on which to base an affirmative answer. There is no reason to expect the court annalists to present Tassilo's case in a favorable light. There is, furthermore, no reason to doubt them when they say that on two occasions favorable to the kings the Frankish rulers forced Tassilo, at the earlier date the young son and heir of a rebellious duke, at the later date a pretentious and rebellious duke in his own right, to commend himself into vassalage, that is, to undergo a ceremony which would demonstrate in a spectacular fashion the Frankish hegemony over Bavaria.

This highly unusual procedure is hardly the basis then for a general description of vassalage. Granting the validity of the commendation into vassalage of 757, we can apply to it as well as to that of 787 the remarks which Krawinkel, having set aside as a fabrication that of 757, applies only to the affair of 787: "Aber aus dieser Tatsache, einer einmaligen und zudem für die Zeit untypischen Episode, unmittelbarer Folge des Krieges, der Niederlage gegenüber einem überwältigenden militärischen Aufgebot, und der Demütigungsabsicht weittragende Schlüsse zu ziehen, in dem Formalakt der Rückverleihung die Verschmelzung von Benefizium und Vasallität als Typus zu er-

VASSI AND FIDELES

blicken, erscheint uns als unzulässige Übertragung von Formen hoch politischer Geschehnisse auf die breite Masse der Benefizien, als eine unzulässige Verallgemeinerung und als ein Überspitzung der juristischen Dogmatik." [441] With the question of benefices we have naught to do here; so far as vassalage is concerned, we can agree heartily with Krawinkel as to the singularity of Tassilo's vassalage.

APPENDIX V

FUSTEL DE COULANGES ON FIDELES

A RATHER different usage of *fideles* is suggested by Fustel de Coulanges who asserts that beginning with the reign of Louis the Pious the council of the king is ordinarily called the "council of the *fideles*."[442] It would seem that this should not be interpreted as meaning that the term *fideles* is then first applied generally to all men in the service of the king, for Fustel de Coulanges himself clearly traces this "narrow sense" of *fideles*, as he says, back at least to Merovingian times.[443] He has in mind not all who serve the king but a still narrower group of inner councillors as opposed to all the men who would appear at general assemblies. These inner councillors would be the leading men of the realm. Fustel de Coulanges says that both before and after the time of Louis the Pious they may be called *optimates, proceres, primores*; beginning with Louis the Pious, they may also be called *fideles*.

This use, however, is not as late as Fustel de Coulanges suggests; the term *fideles* appears earlier in contexts where it must mean men whose advice or opinion the king actually obtains. For example, Charlemagne issued in 769 or a little later a capitulary on behalf of the church "at the urging of the Apostolic See and of all his *fideles*, especially his bishops and other clergy."[444]

It seems to me that Fustel de Coulanges was unnecessarily forcing upon the term *fideles* a newer and narrower meaning than that of faithful servant. The actual advisers of the king would inevitably be important men of the realm (*optimates, proceres, primores*) and at the same time they would be faithful servants of the king who like vassals could be called *fideles*.[445] Fustel de Coulanges himself believed that the usage of the term *fidelis* for faithful servant was established throughout the Carolingian period.[446] There is no use of *fidelis* in the period beginning with Louis the Pious which demands a new connotation for the term such as Fustel de Coulanges suggests; the instances he cites can be read without recourse to a supposedly new and still narrower meaning than that of faithful servant.

APPENDIX VI

BIBLIOGRAPHY

A. SOURCES

1. GUIDES TO THE SOURCES

Dahlmann-Waitz, *Quellenkunde der deutschen Geschichte* (9th ed., Leipzig, 1931).

Auguste Molinier, *Les sources de l'histoire de France*, I, *Des origines aux guerres d'Italie* (Paris, 1901).

W. Wattenbach, *Deutschlands Geschichtsquellen im Mittelalter*, I (7th ed., revised by Ernst Dümmler, Stuttgart and Berlin, 1904).

2. GENERAL COLLECTIONS

Ph. Jaffé, ed., *Bibliotheca Rerum Germanicarum*, 6 vols. (Berlin, 1864–1873).

J. P. Migne, ed., *Patrologiae Cursus Completus, Patrologia Latina*, 221 vols. (Paris, 1844–1864). Cited as Migne, *PL*.

Jean Mabillon, ed., *Vetera Analecta* (2nd ed., Paris, 1723).

Monumenta Germaniae Historica, published by the Gesellschaft für ältere deutsche Geschichtskunde, Hannover and Leipzig, beginning in 1826. Cited as *MGH*, except for the part entitled *Scriptores*, which is cited simply as *SS*.

Recueil des historiens des Gaules et de la France, 24 vols. (Paris, 1738–1904). Cited as *HF*.

3. CONCILIA AND ACTA SANCTORUM

J. D. Mansi and others, ed., *Sacrorum Conciliorum Nova et Amplissima Collectio*, 31 vols. (Florence and Venice, 1759–1798). Cited as Mansi.

MGH, Concilia, I, *Concilia Aevi Merovingici*, edited by Fridericus Maassen (Hannover, 1893).

MGH, Concilia, II, *Concilia Aevi Karolini*, edited by Albert Werminghoff (Hannover and Leipzig, 1906–1908). Cited as *Concilia* (Werminghoff), II. Replaces Mansi for the Frankish councils, 742–840.

Acta Sanctorum, edited by the Bollandists, still in course of publication; Antwerp, 1643-1786; Tongerloo, 1794; Bruxelles, 1845-. Cited as *AA. SS.*

4. CAPITULARIA

MGH, Capitularia Regum Francorum, I, edited by Alfred Boretius; II, edited by Alfred Boretius and Victor Krause (Hannover, 1883-1897). Cited as *Capitularia* (Boretius), I; and *Capitularia* (Krause), II.

5. DIPLOMATA

a. *Regnum Francorum*

Pepin, Carloman, Charlemagne, *MGH, Diplomata Karolinorum*, I (Hannover, 1906).

Louis the Pious, *HF*, VI, 455-632.

b. *Francia Occidentalis*

Charles the Bald, *HF*, VIII, 427-674.

Louis II, *HF*, IX, 398-417.

Carloman, *HF*, IX, 418-438.

Eudes, *HF*, IX, 440-466.

c. *Francia Orientalis*

Louis the German, Carloman, Louis the Young, *MGH, Diplomata Regum Germaniae ex Stirpe Karolinorum*, I (Berlin, 1932-1934).

Charles the Fat, *MGH, Diplomata Regum Germaniae ex Stirpe Karolinorum*, II (Berlin, 1937).

Arnulf, *HF*, IX, 364-369.

d. *Lorraine and Italy*

Lothair I, *HF*, VIII, 365-395.

Lothair II, *HF*, VIII, 404-413.

Louis II, *HF*, VIII, 415-416.

I Diplomi di Guido e di Lamberto, edited by Luigi Schiaparelli (*Fonti per la storia d'Italia*, XXXVI, Rome, 1906).

I Diplomi Berengario I, edited by Luigi Schiaparelli (*Fonti per la storia d'Italia*, XXXV, Rome, 1903).

e. *Aquitaine*

Pepin I, *HF*, VI, 663-680.

Pepin II, *HF*, VIII, 355-363.

f. *Provence*

Recueil des actes des rois de Provence (855-928), edited by René Poupardin (Paris, 1920).

g. *Miscellaneous*

Codex Diplomaticus Alemanniae et Burgundiae Trans-Iuranae, edited by P. Trudpertus Neugart, I (Typis San-Blasianis, 1791).

Die Traditionen des Hochstifts Freising, edited by Theodor Bitterauf, 2 vols. (Munich, 1905–1909).

6. FORMULAE

MGH, Formulae Merowingici et Karolini Aevi, edited by Karl Zeumer, I (two parts, Hannover, 1882–1886).

Chartae Ludovici Pii, HF, VI, 633–661.

Quaedam Notitiae et Chartae (late ninth and tenth centuries), *HF,* IX, 705–736.

Das Formelbuch des Bischofs Salomo III von Konstanz, edited by Ernst Dümmler (Leipzig, 1857).

7. EPISTOLAE

a. *Kings*

Charlemagne, Jaffé, *Bibliotheca Rerum Germanicarum,* IV, 335–436.

Louis the Pious, *HF,* VI, 333–350; Migne, *PL,* CIV, 1309–1332.

Charles the Bald, Migne, *PL,* CXXIV, 861–896.

Lothair II of Lorraine, *HF,* VII, 567–571.

Louis II of Italy, *HF,* VII, 572–578.

b. *Popes*

Hadrian I (died in 795), Migne, *PL,* XCVI, 1203–1242.

Leo III (died in 816), *HF,* V, 597–604; Migne, *PL,* CII, 1023–1068; Jaffé, *Bibliotheca Rerum Germanicarum,* IV, 308–334.

Paschal I (died in 824), Migne, *PL,* CII, 1085–1094.

Gregory IV (died in 844), Migne, *PL,* CVI, 853–862.

Leo IV (died in 855), *MGH, Epistolae,* V, 585–612.

Benedict III (died in 858), Migne, *PL,* CXV, 689–702.

Nicholas I (died in 867), *HF,* VII, 385–438; Migne, *PL,* CXIX, 769–1182.

Hadrian II (died in 872), *HF,* VII, 439–458; Migne, *PL,* CXXII, 1259–1320.

John VIII (died in 882), *HF,* VII, 459–479; *HF,* IX, 157–198; Migne, *PL,* CXXVI, 651–966; *MGH, Epistolae,* VII, 1–333.

Marinus I (died in 884), *HF,* IX, 198–199; Migne, *PL,* CXXVI, 967–970.

APPENDIX VI 101

Hadrian III (died in 885), Migne, *PL*, CXXVI, 971–974.
Stephan V (died in 891), Migne, *PL*, CXXIX, 785–822.
Formosus (died in 896), Migne, *PL*, CXXIX, 837–854.
Stephan VI (died in 897), Migne, *PL*, CXXIX, 855–860.
Romanus (died in 897), Migne, *PL*, CXXIX, 859–862.
John IX (died in 900), Migne, *PL*, CXXXI, 27–38.
Epistolae Selectae Pontificum Romanorum, Carolo Magno et Ludovico Pio Regnantibus Scriptae, *MGH*, *Epistolae*, V, 1–84.
Epistolae Summorum Pontificum (882–996) *HF*, IX, 157–253.

c. *Others*

Agobard, archbishop of Lyon (died in 840), *MGH*, *Epistolae*, V, 150–239.
Alcuin of York (died in 804), *MGH*, *Epistolae*, IV, 1–481.
Aldricus, abbot of Ferrières, archbishop of Sens (died in 836), Migne, *PL*, CV, 809–814.
Amalarius, archbishop of Trèves (died after 850), *MGH*, *Epistolae*, V, 240–274.
Boniface (died in 754) and Lull (died in 786), *MGH*, *Epistolae*, III, 231–431.
Einhard, Jaffé, *Bibliotheca Rerum Germanicarum*, IV, 437–486; *MGH*, *Epistolae*, V, 105–145.
Frotharius, abbot of Saint-Evre, bishop of Toul (died in 849 or 850), *MGH*, *Epistolae*, V, 275–298.
Hincmar, archbishop of Rheims (died in 882), Migne, *PL*, CXXV, CXXVI. Many more known to Flodoard analyzed in *lib*. III of his *Historiae Ecclesiae Remensis Libri Quatuor*, *SS*, XIII, 405–599.
Hincmar, bishop of Laon (died before 882), Migne, *PL*, CXXIV, 979–1072; CXXVI, 279–648.
Loup, abbot of Ferrières (died shortly after 862), edited by Léon Levillain (*Les classiques de l'histoire de France au moyen âge*), 2 vols. (Paris, 1927–1935).
Paul the Deacon (died *ca*. 800), *MGH*, *Epistolae*, IV, 505–516.
Rabanus Maurus Magnentius, abbot of Fulda, archbishop of Mainz (died in 856), *MGH*, *Epistolae*, V, 379–533.
Epistolae Variorum Carolo Magno Regnante Scriptae, *MGH*, *Epistolae*, IV, 494–567.
Epistolae Variorum, Inde a Morte Carolo Magni Usque ad

Divisionem Imperii, Collectae, MGH, Epistolae, V, 299–360, 615–640.
Epistolae Variorum Inde a Saeculo Nono Medio Usque ad Mortem Karoli II (Calvi), MGH, Epistolae, VI, 127–206.
Variorum Epistolae (reign of Charles the Bald), *HF*, VII, 579–597.
Variorum Epistolae (ninth and tenth centuries), *HF*, IX, 293–299.

8. ANNALES

Annales Laurissenses Minores, SS, I, 114–123. Covers the period from Pepin of Heristal to 817.
Annales Regni Francorum (Annales Laurissenses Maiores et Einhardi), edited by Fridericus Kurze (*Scriptores Rerum Germanicarum in Usum Scholarum*, Hannover, 1895). Covers the years 741–829.
Annales Bertiniani, edited by G. Waitz (*Scriptores Rerum Germanicarum in Usum Scholarum*, Hannover, 1883). Covers the years 741–882.
Annales Fuldenses, edited by Fridericus Kurze (*Scriptores Rerum Germanicarum in Usum Scholarum*, Hannover, 1891). Covers the years 714–901.
Annales Vedastini, SS, I, 517–531; *SS*, II, 196–209. Covers the years 874–900.
Lesser Carolingian annals, collected in *SS*, I, 1–111; II, 184–259. Indicated at greater length by Auguste Molinier, *Les sources de l'histoire de France*, I (Paris, 1901), nos. 684–743.

9. OTHER LITERARY SOURCES

Acta Elevationis S. Agricolae, Cabilonensis Episcopi, et Aliorum Beatorum (877–878; dates from before the end of the ninth century), *AA. SS.*, March, II, 515–516.
Actus Pontificum Cenomannis in Urbe Degentium, edited by Johannes Mabillon, *Vetera Analecta* (new edition, Paris, 1723), pp. 239–338; edited by G. Busson and A. Ledru (*Société des archives historiques du Maine*, Le Mans, 1901). Concerning the dates of the various parts, see Julien Havet, *Oeuvres* (Paris, 1896), I, 318 ff.
Adrevaldus, monk of Fleury (died in 878 or 879), *Miracula S. Benedicti*, Migne, *PL*, CXXIV, 909–948.

APPENDIX VI 103

Agobard, archbishop of Lyon (died in 840), *Liber Apologeticus pro Filiis Ludowici*, SS, XV, pt. I, 274-279.

Aldricus, *Gesta Aldrici Episcopi Cenomanensis* (832-857), Migne, *PL*, CXV, 29-106; SS, XV, 308-325; edited by R. Charles and L. Froger (Mamers, 1889).

Altfridus (died in 859), *Vita S. Liudgeri Episcopi Mimigardensis (Monasteriensis)* (died in 809), SS, II, 403-419.

Anskarius, archbishop of Bremen-Hamburg, *Vita S. Willehadi Bremensis Episcopi* (died in 789), SS, II, 378-390. Written a little after 838.

Chronicarum Quae Dicuntur Fredegarii Scholastici Libri IV cum Continuationibus, MGH, *Scriptores Rerum Merovingicarum*, II, 1-193. The continuation by Nibelungus covers the period 753-768; *op. cit.*, II, 182-193.

Ebbo, archbishop of Rheims, *Apologeticum* (840), Migne, *PL*, CXVI, 11-16.

Eigil, abbot of Fulda (818-822), *Vita S. Sturmi Fuldensis Abbatis* (died in 779), SS, II, 365-377.

Einhard, *Vita Caroli Magni*, edited by G. Waitz (*Scriptores Rerum Germanicarum in Usum Scholarum*, 5th ed., Hannover and Leipzig, 1905).

Erchempertus, monk of Monte Cassino, *Historia Langobardorum Beneventum Degentium* (774-889), SS, III, 240-264. Written after 883.

Ermoldus Nigellus, cleric attached to service of Pepin I of Aquitaine, *In Honorem Hludovici Libri Quatuor*, SS, II, 464-523; *MGH*, *Poetae Latini*, II, 5-91.

Flodoard, canon of Rheims (died in 966), *Historiae Ecclesiae Remensis Libri Quatuor*, SS, XIII, 405-599. This dates from a later time than our period but it contains numerous references to letters of Hincmar of Rheims and digests of the contents of many of them.

Florus of Lyon (died *ca*. 860), *Querela de Divisione Imperii*, Migne, *PL*, CXIX, 249-256; *MGH*, *Poetae Latini*, II, 555-564.

Gesta Abbatum Fontanellensium, SS, II, 270-301. Written 833-845.

Gregory of Tours (died in 595) *Historia Francorum*, edited by

René Poupardin (*Collection des textes pour servir à l'étude . . . de l'histoire*, Paris, 1913).
Herard, archbishop of Tours (856–869), *Vita S. Chrodegandi Sagiensis Episcopi* (died *ca.* 770), *AA. SS.*, September, I, 768.
Hincmar, archbishop of Rheims (died in 882), *Opera*, Migne, *PL*, CXXV, CXXVI.
Hincmar, archbishop of Rheims, *De Ordine Palatii, Capitularia* (Krause), II, 517–530; translated into French and edited by Maurice Prou (Paris, 1884).
Jonas of Orleans (died in 843), *De Institutione Laicali, Opusculum de Institutione Regia*, Migne, *PL*, CVI, 121–306; Jean Reviron, *Les idées politico-religieuses d'un évêque du IXe siècle, Jonas d'Orléans et son "De institutione regia"* (Paris 1930).
Monk of St. Gall, *De Gestis Caroli Magni Libri Duo* (written between 884–887), Jaffé, *Bibliotheca Rerum Germanicarum*, IV, 628–700; *SS*, II, 726–763.
Narratio Clericorum Remensium (835–851, written 853), Migne, *PL*, CXVI, 17–22.
Nithard, *Historiarum Libri IV*, *SS*, II, 649–672; *Histoire des fils de Louis le Pieux*, edited by Ph. Lauer (*Les classiques de l'histoire de France au moyen âge*, Paris, 1926).
Paul the Deacon (died *ca.* 800), *Historia Langobardorum*, edited by G. Waitz (*Scriptores Rerum Germanicarum in Usum Scholarum*, Hannover, 1878).
Paul the Deacon, *Gesta Episcoporum Mettensium* (written *ca.* 784), *SS*, II, 260–268.
Poeta Saxo, Vita Karoli Magni (composed between 888 and 891), *SS*, I, 227–279; Jaffé, *Bibliotheca Rerum Germanicarum*, IV, 544–627.
Radbertus Paschasius, abbot of Corbie (died *ca.* 865), *Epitaphium Arsenii* (also known as *Vita Walae*), edited by Ernst Dümmler (*Abhandlungen der königlichen Akademie der Wissenschaften zu Berlin*, 1899–1900).
Radbertus Paschasius, abbot of Corbie (died *ca.* 865), *Vita S. Adalardi* (died in 826), Migne, *PL*, CXX, 1507–1556.
Ratpertus, Monk of St. Gall (died *ca.* 900), *Casus S. Galli* (*ca.* 570–883), *SS*, II, 59–74.

APPENDIX VI 105

Rimbert, archbishop of Bremen-Hamburg (died in 888), *Vita S. Anskarii Hammaburgensis Episcopi* (died in 865), *SS*, II, 683-725; edited by G. Waitz (*Scriptores Rerum Germanicarum in Usum Scholarum*, Hannover, 1884).

Ruodolfus, monk of Fulda, *Vita S. Leobae Abbatissae Bischofheimensis* (died in 782 or 783), *SS*, XV, 121-131. Written before 838.

Sedulius Scotus (last mentioned in 858), *De Rectoribus Christianis*, Migne, *PL*, CIII, 291-332.

Smaragdus, abbot of Saint-Mihiel (died *ca.* 830), *Via Regia*, Migne, *PL*, CII, 931-970.

Thegan, *Vita Hludowici Imperatoris*, *SS*, II, 585 ff. Written *ca.* 837.

Vita Aldrici, abbot of Ferrières, archbishop of Sens (died in 836), Migne, *PL*, CV, 799-810. Composed in late ninth or early tenth century.

Vita S. Barnardi Viennensis Archiepiscopi (died *ca.* 842), *AA. SS.*, January, II, 545-547; *Anal. Bolland.*, XI, 404-415.

Vita Hludowici Imperatoris (by an anonymous person sometimes called the Astronomer), *SS*, II, 604-648. Written *ca.* 840.

Vita Sanctae Liutbirgae (died *ca.* 870), *SS*, IV, 158-164. Written shortly after her death.

Vita S. Rimberti, archbishop of Bremen-Hamburg (died in 888), *SS*, II, 764-775. Written by a pupil or friend of Rimbert.

Walafrid Strabo, *Libellus de Exordiis et Incrementis Rerum Ecclesiasticarum* (written 840-842), *Capitularia* (Krause), II, 473-516.

B. SECONDARY WORKS

Abel, Sigurd, *Jahrbücher des fränkischen Reiches unter Karl dem Grossen*, I (2nd ed. revised by Bernhard Simson, Leipzig, 1888); II (by Bernhard Simson, Leipzig, 1883).

Beaudouin, Édouard, "La recommendation et la justice seigneuriale," *Annales de l'enseignement supérieur de Grenoble*, I (1889), 35-133.

Bloch, Marc, *La société féodale, la formation des liens de dépendance* (Paris, 1939).

Böhmer, Johann Friedrich, *Die Regesten des Kaiserreichs, 751–918* (2nd ed. revised by Engelbert Mühlbacher, Innsbruck, 1908).
Breysig, Theodor, *Jahrbücher des fränkischen Reiches, 714–741* (Leipzig, 1869).
Brunner, Heinrich, *Deutsche Rechtsgeschichte,* I (2nd ed., Leipzig, 1906); II (2nd ed. revised by Claudius Freiherr von Schwerin, Munich and Leipzig, 1928). Cited as Brunner with appropriate volume and page.
Calmette, Joseph, *La diplomatie carolingienne, 843–877* (Paris, 1901).
Calmette, J., *La société féodale* (4th edition, Paris, 1938).
Cambridge Medieval History, II, III (New York, 1913–1922).
Chénon, E., *Histoire générale du droit français public et privé,* I (Paris, 1926).
Dahn, Felix, *Die Könige der Germanen,* VII, pt. 1–3, *Die Franken unter den Merovingen* (Leipzig, 1894–1895); VIII, pts. 1–6, *Die Franken unter den Karolingen* (Leipzig, 1897–1899).
Declareuil, J., *Histoire général du droit français* (Paris, 1925).
Dopsch, Alfons, *Die Wirtschaftsentwicklung der Karolingerzeit,* 2 volumes (2nd ed., Weimar, 1921–1922).
Dopsch, Alfons, *Wirtschaftliche und soziale Grundlagen der europäischen Kulturentwicklung,* 2 volumes (2nd ed., Vienna, 1923–1924).
Dopsch, Alfons, "Beneficialwesen und Feudalität," *Mitteilungen des Österreichischen Instituts für Geschichtsforschung,* XLVI (1932), 1–36.
Dümmler, Ernst, *Geschichte des ostfränkischen Reiches,* 3 volumes (2nd ed., Leipzig, 1887–1888).
Dumas, Auguste, "Encore la question: 'Fidèles ou vassaux?'," *Nouvelle revue historique de droit français et étranger,* XLIV (1920), 159–229, 347–390.
Dumas, Auguste, "Le serment de fidélité et la conception du pouvoir du Ier au IXe siècle," *Revue historique de droit français et étranger,* 4e série, X (1931), 30–51, 289–321.
Dumas, Auguste, "Le serment de fidélité à l'époque franque, Réponse à M. Ferdinand Lot," *Revue belge de philologie et d'histoire,* XIV (1935), 405–426.

APPENDIX VI 107

Ehrenberg, Victor, *Commendation und Huldigung nach fränkischen Recht* (Weimar, 1877).
Esmein, A., *Cours élémentaire d'histoire du droit français* (15th edition revised by R. Génestal, Paris, 1925).
Favre, Édouard, *Eudes comte de Paris et roi de France, 882-898* (Paris, 1893).
Fustel de Coulanges, *La monarchie franque* (Paris, 1888).
Fustel de Coulanges, *Les origines du système féodal, Le bénéfice et le patronat pendant l'époque mérovingienne* (Paris, 1890).
Fustel de Coulanges, *Les transformations de la royauté pendant l'époque carolingienne* (Paris, 1892).
Gams, P. B., *Series Episcoporum Ecclesiae Catholicae* (2nd ed., Leipzig, 1931).
Ganshof, F. L., "Note sur les origines de l'union du bénéfice avec la vassalité," *Études d'histoire dédiées à la mémoire de Henri Pirenne par ses anciens élèves* (Bruxelles, 1937), pp. 173-189.
Ganshof, F. L., "Benefice and Vassalage in the Age of Charlemagne," *Cambridge Historical Journal*, VI (1939), 147-175.
Goebel, Julius, Jr., *Felony and Misdemeanor, A Study in the History of English Criminal Procedure*, I (New York, 1937). Deals with Frankish origins.
Guilhiermoz, P., *Essai sur l'origine de la noblesse en France au moyen âge* (Paris, 1902). Cited as Guilhiermoz.
Hahn, Heinrich, *Jahrbücher des fränkischen Reichs, 741-752* (Berlin, 1863).
Halphen, Louis, *Études critiques sur l'histoire de Charlemagne* (Paris, 1921).
Halphen, Louis, *Les barbares, des grandes invasions aux conquêtes turques du XIe siècle* (volume V in the series *Peuples et Civilisations* edited by Louis Halphen and Philippe Sagnac, 3rd ed., Paris, 1936).
Halphen, Louis, *L'Essor de l'Europe* (vol. VI in the same *Peuples et Civilisations* series, Paris, 1932).
Hauck, Albert, *Kirchengeschichte Deutschlands*, II (1st ed., Leipzig, 1890).
Havet, Julien, *Oeuvres*, 2 vols., (Paris, 1896).

Hefele, Charles Joseph, *Histoire des conciles*, French translation of second German edition revised by Dom H. Leclerq, III, pt. 2 (Paris, 1910); IV, pt. 1 (Paris, 1911).

Holtzmann, Robert, *Französische Verfassungsgeschichte von der Mitte des neunten Jahrhunderts bis zur Revolution* (Munich and Berlin, 1910).

Imbart de la Tour, Pierre, *Les élections épiscopales dans l'église de France du IXe au XIIe siècle* (Paris, 1891).

Kleinclausz, Arthur, *Charlemagne* (Paris, 1934).

Kleinclausz, Arthur, *L'empire carolingien, ses origines et ses transformations* (Paris, 1902).

Krawinkel, Hermann, *Untersuchungen zum fränkischen Benefizialrecht* (Weimar, 1937).

Lavisse, Ernest, ed., *Histoire de France depuis les origines jusqu'à la révolution*, II, pt. I, *Le Christianisme, Les barbares mérovingiens et carolingiens* (by C. Bayet, C. Pfister and A. Kleinclausz, Paris, 1903).

Lesne, Émile, *Histoire de la propriété ecclésiastique en France*, I (Lille, 1910); II, pt. 1 (Lille, 1922); II, pt. 2 (Lille, 1926); II, pt. 3 (Lille, 1928); III (Lille, 1936).

Lot, Ferdinand, *Fidèles ou vassaux?* (Paris, 1904).

Lot, Ferdinand, "Le serment de fidélité à l'époque franque," *Revue belge de philologie et d'histoire*, XII (1933), 569–582.

Lot, Ferdinand, and Louis Halphen, *Le règne de Charles le Chauve* (Paris, 1909). Only the first part covering the years 840–851 has appeared.

Lot, Ferdinand, Christian Pfister, and François L. Ganshof, *Les destinées de l'empire en occident de 395 à 888* (vol. I of *Histoire du moyen âge*, part of the *Histoire générale* being published under the direction of Gustave Glotz, Paris, 1928–1935).

Manitius, M., *Geschichte der lateinischen Literatur des Mittelalters*, I (Munich, 1911); II (Munich, 1923).

Mayer, Ernst, *Deutsche und französische Verfassungsgeschichte vom 9. bis zum 14. Jahrhundert*, 2 vols. (Leipzig, 1899).

Mitteis, Heinrich, *Lehnrecht und Staatsgewalt* (Weimar, 1933).

Odegaard, C. E., "Carolingian Oaths of Fidelity," *Speculum*, XVI (1941), 284–296.

APPENDIX VI

Oelsner, Ludwig, *Jahrbücher des fränkischen Reiches unter König Pippin* (Leipzig, 1871).
Parisot, Robert, *Le royaume de Lorraine sous les carolingiens 843-923* (Paris, 1898).
Petot, Pierre, "L'hommage servile," *Revue historique de droit français et étranger*, 4e série, VI (1927), 68-107.
Pöschl, Arnold, *Bischofsgut und Mensa Episcopalis*, 3 vols. (Bonn, 1908-1912).
Poupardin, René, *Le royaume de Provence sous les Carolingiens, 855-933* (Paris, 1901).
Roth, Paul, *Feudalität und Unterthanverband* (Weimar, 1863).
Roth, Paul, *Geschichte des Beneficialwesens* (Erlangen, 1850).
Schröder, Richard, and Eberhard Frhr. v. Kunssberg, *Lehrbuch der deutschen Rechtsgeschichte* (7th ed., Berlin and Leipzig, 1932).
Schrörs, Heinrich, *Hinkmar Erzbischof von Reims* (Freiburg-im-Breisgau, 1884).
Simson, Bernhard, *Die Entstehung der Pseudo-Isidorischen Fälschungen in Le Mans* (Leipzig, 1886).
Simson, Bernhard, *Jahrbücher des fränkischen Reichs unter Ludwig dem Frommen*, 2 vols. (Leipzig, 1874-1876).
Stephenson, Carl, "The Origin and Significance of Feudalism," *American Historical Review*, XLVI (1941), 788-812.
Stutz, Ulrich, " 'Römerwergeld' und 'Herrenfall'," *Abhandlungen der preussischen Akademie der Wissenschaften, Philosophisch-historische Klasse*, 1934.
Stutz, Ulrich, "Lehen und Pfrunde," *Zeitschrift der Savignystiftung für Rechtsgeschichte, Germanistische Abteilung*, XX (1879), 213-247.
Viollet, Paul, *Histoire des institutions politiques et administratives de la France*, I (Paris, 1890).
Voigt, Karl, *Staat und Kirche von Konstantin dem Grossen bis zum Ende der Karolingerzeit* (Stuttgart, 1936).
Waitz, Georg, *Deutsche Verfassungsgeschichte*, I (3rd. ed., Berlin, 1880); II (3rd ed., Berlin, 1882); III (2nd ed., Berlin, 1883); IV (2nd ed., Berlin, 1885). Cited as Waitz with appropriate volume and page.
Waitz, Georg, "Über die Anfänge der Vassallität," *Gesammelte Abhandlungen* (edited by Karl Zeumer, Göttingen, 1896), 178-259.

NOTES

PREFACE

[1] F. Funck-Brentano, *The Middle Ages* (London, 1926), p. 3.

[2] See the deserved strictures upon historians who in dealing with institutions use pell-mell sources from widely separated periods in Julius Goebel, *Felony and Misdemeanor*, I (New York, 1937), 125, n. 3; 190, n. 4.

CHAPTER I

[1] See F. Lot, "Le serment de fidélité," *Rev. belge de philol. et d'hist.*, XII (1933), 569; Marc Bloch, *La société féodale, la formation des liens de dépendance* (Paris, 1939), pp. 233–237.

[2] The significance of these ceremonies, that is, entrance into service, is not disputed; there is some disagreement as to which of the two ceremonies, commendation or the oath of fidelity, is the most "essential" or most "important" part, and as to the absolute necessity of both ceremonies in order to establish a service relationship; see Appendix I. For the sake of brevity I shall refer to this entrance into service as commendation without always mentioning the oath of fidelity which frequently followed the actual ceremony of commendation.

The best recent account of commendation is that by F. Lot in F. Lot, C. Pfister, and F. L. Ganshof, *Les destinées de l'empire en occident de 395 à 888* (Paris, 1928–1934; vol. I of *Histoire du moyen âge*, ed. Gustave Glotz), pp. 641–677. The literature on this subject is very extensive; for example, P. Roth, *Geschichte des Beneficialwesens* (Erlangen, 1850), pp. 378–386, *passim*; P. Roth, *Feudalität und Unterthanverband* (Weimar, 1863), pp. 208–209, 266–280; V. Ehrenberg, *Commendation und Huldigung* (Weimar, 1877); Waitz (see Abbreviations), II, pt. I, 330 ff.; Waitz, IV, 233 ff.; J. Flach, *Les origines de l'ancienne France*, I (Paris, 1886), 79 ff.; Fustel de Coulanges, *Les origines du système féodal* (Paris, 1890), pp. 192–332; Guilhiermoz (see Abbreviations), pp. 78–85; Brunner (see Abbreviations), II, 66 ff., 362–365; A. Dopsch, *Wirtschaftliche und soziale Grundlagen der europäischen Kulturentwicklung* (2nd ed., Wien, 1923–1924), II, 304–306; Bloch, *La société féodale, les liens de dépendance*, pp. 223 ff.

[3] Two priests, Jacob and Simon, enter the service of Hitto, bishop of Freising, in 815; Theodor Bitterauf, *Die Traditionen des Hochstifts Freising*, I (Munich, 1905), 295, No. 345; cited incompletely by Waitz, IV, 246, n. 5.

NOTES

⁴ Many texts in Guilhiermoz, p. 82, n. 12.

⁵ Guilhiermoz, p. 79, n. 5; p. 80, n. 8.

⁶ Capitulary of Pepin, son of Charlemagne, at Pavia, 787, *Capitularia* (Boretius), I, 200, c. 13: "Stetit nobis de illos liberos Langobardos, ut licentiam habeant se commendandi ubi voluerint, *si commendatus non est*, sicut a tempore Langobardorum fecerunt, in tantum ut suo comiti faciat rationabiliter quod debet." One of the manuscripts reads in place of the clause in italics *si seniorem non habuerit*. Not to be a *commendatus* is not to have a seignior. The manuscript which reads *si seniorem non habuerit* is Boretius' No. 7, the *Codex S. Pauli in Karinthia* $XXV\frac{a}{4}$ which dates from 817–823; see *Capitularia* (Krause), II, xxvi. Among the other manuscripts, all of which read *si commendatus non est*, is Boretius' No. 6, the *Codex Eporediensis* 34, which dates from *circa* 830; see *Capitularia* (Krause), II, xv.

⁷ *Capitularia* (Boretius), I, 165, c. 7: "Sunt etiam alii qui dicunt se esse *homines* Pippini et Chluduici et tunc profitentur se ire *ad servitium dominorum suorum*, quando alii pagenses in exercitum pergere debent. c. 8. Sunt iterum et alii qui remanent et dicunt, quod *seniores* eorum domi resideant et debeant cum eorum *senioribus* pergere, ubicumque iussio domni imperatoris fuerit. Alii vero sunt *qui ideo se commendant ad aliquos seniores, quos sciunt in hostem non profecturos.*" My italics. *Homines* are men who have commended themselves; this matter is discussed below.

⁸ For other texts see Waitz, IV, 244, n. 1; Fustel de Coulanges, *Transformations de la royauté pendant l'époque carolingienne* (Paris, 1892), p. 602.

⁹ Letter of Einhard, *MGH, Epistolae*, V, 126, No. 34: "Eum suscipere dignemini, et quando in vestras manus se commendaverit, aliquam consolationem ei faciatis de beneficiis." Other examples, n. 201 and n. 224. See Guilhiermoz, p. 83, n. 13.

¹⁰ Fustel de Coulanges, *Transformations*, p. 606: "Il a donc deux sortes de sujets: à titre de roi et d'empereur, il est un chef d'État; à titre de seigneur et de patron, il est un chef de vassaux."

¹¹ *Cambridge Medieval History*, II, 151. Similar remarks by Pfister in Ernest Lavisse, editor, *Histoire de France*, II¹ (Paris, 1903), 200. Marc Bloch, *La société féodale, les liens de dépendance* (Paris, 1939), pp. 224–225, describes the ceremony of commendation and then adds: "Pour désigner le supérieur, qu'elle créait, point d'autres termes que le nom, très général, de 'seigneur.' Souvent, le subordonné est dit de même, sans plus, 'l'homme' de ce seigneur. Quelquefois, avec plus de précision, son 'homme de bouche et de mains.' Mais on emploie aussi des mots mieux spécialisés: 'vassal' ou, jusqu'au début du XIIe siècle au moins, 'commendé.'" René Poupardin in *Cambridge Medieval History*, III, 54.

¹² Paul Viollet, *Histoire des institutions politiques* (Paris, 1890), I, 429:

"L'acte par lequel un homme se constitue le *vassus* d'un *senior*, est la recommendation, *commendare, se commendare*. On dit aussi *se tradere*."
Robert Holtzmann, *Französische Verfassungsgeschichte* (Munich and Berlin, 1910), p. 11: "der, welcher sich kommendiert wird *vassus* (etwas später auch *vassallus*—das Wort ist wahrscheinlich keltischen Ursprungs) oder *homo* genannt, der andere ist sein *senior* (*seigneur*) oder *dominus*." Holtzmann applies this to the period from 843 to 1180.

A. Esmein, *Cours élémentaire d'histoire du droit français* (15th ed., by R. Génestal, Paris, 1925), pp. 113, 114: "Les textes nous disent d'eux (les *vassi* du roi) qu'ils ont solonnellement juré fidélité au roi en mettant leurs mains dans les siennes, ce qui est habituellement indiqué par l'expression *sese commendaverunt*." Also p. 189: "vassalité ou *commendatio* de la Monarchie Franque."

Émile Chénon, *Histoire générale du droit français public et privé*, I (Paris, 1926), 480: "l'homme recommandé s'appelait *commendatus, susceptus*, et à partir du VIIIe siècle *vassus* ou *vassallus*"; also p. 290.

Pierre Petot, "L'hommage servile," *Rev. hist. du droit français et étranger*, 4e série, VI (1927), 91–92: "L'homme libre qui se commande se subordonne à autrui; on le qualifie désormais de *vassus*."

Ulrich Stutz, "Römerwergeld und Herrenfall," *Abh. der preus. Akad. der Wiss.*, 1934, no. 2., p. 55; entrance into vassalage effected by a double ceremony; *homagium* or commendation and the swearing of an oath of fidelity. For a discussion of the relationship between these two ceremonies, see my Appendix I.

F. L. Ganshof, "Note sur les origines de l'union du bénéfice avec la vassalité," *Études d'histoire dédiées à la mémoire de Henri Pirenne* (Bruxelles, 1937), p. 187: "On y rencontre un *homo francus*, un homme libre, qui a un *senior*; c'est donc un homme, qui s'est 'recommandé,' en d'autres termes un vassal." Also, "Benefice and Vassalage," *Cambridge Historical Journal*, VI (1939), 155.

The ideas of Jacques Flach in *Les origines de l'ancienne France*, I (Paris, 1886), call for a word of explanation because of his rather confusing terminology. He identifies the *commendatus* as a vassal; *ibid.*, I, 81: "Le recommandé (*leude, homo*) (plus tard *vassus*)"; I, 121, n. 1: ". . . la fidélité que les recommandés, les *vassi*, gardent à leur seigneur." One of Flach's fundamental notions is that all the subjects of the Frankish king find in him a protector; hence *all* are in his *recommendation*. Some men, however, receive his special protection in return for services rendered and these latter are in *la recommendation proprement dite*; *ibid.*, I, 86–88. It is to this *recommendation proprement dite*, that is, to what other writers call simply "commendation," that Flach refers in a passage which at first glance seems to imply that vassalage is a special kind of commendation; *ibid.*, I, p. 120, n. 1: "Il faut remarquer seulement que les mots *vassus*, *vassalus, senior, vassaticum,* furent reservés de preférénce aux relations nées de la recommandation proprement dite, telle que nous l'avons vu se constituer au VIIIe siècle."

[13] J. Declareuil, *Histoire générale du droit français* (Paris, 1925), p. 117: "le roi, absolu en tant que roi, était en même temps le plus haut *senior*. Tous les grands, et par conséquent ses agents, étaient ses *vassi*." *Ibid.*, p. 117: "le Prince choisissait ses fonctionnaires parmi ses *vassi.*"

[14] In E. Lavisse, *Histoire de France*, II[1], 420–421.

[15] Henri Pirenne, *Mohammed and Charlemagne* (New York, 1939), p. 272.

[16] *Ibid.*, p. 271, n. 2.

[17] Poupardin frequently refers to great magnates as vassals; *Cambridge Medieval History*, III, 1–70, *passim*; e. g., III, 48 where Lambert, Frankish duke of Spoleto in the time of Louis II of Italy, is an "intractable vassal."

F. L. Ganshof, "Benefice and Vassalage," *Cambridge Historical Journal*, VI (1939), 167, speaks of counts entering "vassalage"; he bases this statement upon a series of texts which show only that counts held benefices of the king. The possession of a benefice may be used as a proof of vassalage; *ibid.*, 171, n. 114. He also interprets the commendation *ad procerem* and oath of fidelity of Bernard, King of Italy, as a declaration of vassalage; *ibid.*, 155, n. 42.

Esmein, *Cours*, p. 131, says that the counts were chosen from among the king's vassals; even after their offices had become hereditary so that they held them by their own right, they had to enter the vassalage of the king.

Viollet speaks of royal functionaries who are vassals, and he includes among *les grands vassaux* Robert the Strong, Count of Autun, Nevers, and Auxerre; and Eudes, Count of Paris, Blois, and Orleans; *Histoire des institutions politiques*, I, 453.

Joseph Calmette, *La société féodale* (4th ed., Paris, 1938), pp. 25–26. Pierre Petot, *Rev. hist. du droit fr. et étr.*, 4e série, VI (1927), 100: "Aux *vassi dominici* le roi confie volontiers des fonctions publiques, même les plus hautes, celle de duc, de comte, ou de *missus dominicus*."

Arnold Pöschl, *Bischofsgut und Mensa Episcopalis*, I (Bonn, 1908), 166, n. 1: "auch der Vassallität assimilierte sich die Stellung der Prälaten zur Krone."

[18] Waitz, IV, 242: "Wer sich commendiert hat, wird vorzugsweise vassus oder vassallus genannt, mit einem Wort, das in den verschiedensten Beziehungen gebraucht wird, für niedere Landbesitzer welche ihre Hufen von einem Stift oder einem andern Herrn empfangen haben, wie für den vornehmen Weltlichen der an den Hof des Königs gebracht ist, den Abt der sich commendiert und seine Abtei vielleicht zu Beneficium empfangen, oder den mächtigen Grossen, den fremden Fürsten, die sich auf besonderen

Gründen in dies Verhältnis (in vassaticum, wie man sagte) begeben haben."

[19] Waitz, IV, 280: "Unter ihm [Pippin] und seinen Nachfolgern haben dann fremde Fürsten, die sich dem Fränkischen König unterwarfen, gleichfalls die vassallitische Huldigung geleistet: bei Sarracenischen in Spanien, Brittischen, Slavischen und Dänischen wird es erwähnt: ein solcher König heisst ausdrücklich Vassus Karls."

[20] The king of the Abodriti, see below p. 68; Waitz, IV, 280, had previously referred to the act of commendation into vassalage of Tassilo; see below p. 47.

[21] Waitz, IV, 280, n. 3.

[22] Waitz, IV, 246, n. 5. The word *militia* in the ninth century was only beginning to get a martial air; it originally meant service of any kind, and could still mean that in the ninth century. See Maurice Prou's edition of Hincmar's *De Ordine Palatii* (Paris, 1884; fasc. 58, *Bibliothèque de l'École des hautes études*), p. 66, n. 2.

[23] Waitz, IV, 282-283: "So ist es begreiflich, wenn auch auf die Stellung der höheren Beamten im Reich die Vassallität Einfluss gewann, diese wohl geradezu als Vassallen behandelt und bezeichnet wurden.... Zuerst vorzüglich bei den Abteien ist es geschehen, die schon immer geradezu als Beneficien verliehen worden sind, deren Vorsteher anderer seits an eine Commendation gewöhnt waren, die sich von der Commendation in die Vassallität an sich nicht unterschied. Aber auch bei Bischöfen kommt es vor, dass sie bei Empfang ihrer Würde sich als Vassallen des Königs bekennen. Doch haben sie bereits im 9ten Jahrhundert der eigentlich vassallitischen Huldigung widerstrebt; und auch der Eid den sie leisteten war abweichend von dem der weltlichen Grossen: er nahm Rücksicht auf das geistliche Amt, enthielt aber wenigstens manchmal daneben der Verpflichtung getreu zu sein wie ein Mann oder Vassall seinem Herrn."

[24] Waitz, IV, 248: "Doch findet es sich bei Geistlichen die in den persönlichen Dienst des Königs traten, bei Bischöfen welche sich ihm commendierten, ohne dass ihr Verhältnis geradezu als das der Vassallität aufgefasst wäre. Wo aber diese begründet werden sollte, war der Treueid feste Regel: er ist immer mehr das Unterscheidende für dies Verhältnis geworden."

[25] Waitz, III, 408: "Dazu kommt in den Beziehungen der Grafen zu den Königen und ebenso der Unterbeamten zu den Grafen oder anderen Herren ein gewisser Einfluss der Vassallitätsverhältnisse, wenn auch zunächst nur so dass häufig Vassallen zu diesen Stellen genommen, später aber auch in der Weise dass beide, Beamte und Vassallen, in mancher Beziehung gleich behandelt werden."

[26] Waitz, III, 301-302: "Selbst die Mitglieder der königlichen Familie müssen solche Eide [oath of fidelity sworn by all subjects of the king] leisten, Söhne dem Vater, Neffen dem Oheim, und wenn sie sich hier mitunter auf besondere Vereinbarungen oder Versprechungen beziehen, so in

NOTES

anderen Fällen auch allgemein auf Treue und Ergebenheit, sie fallen dann aber, ebenso wie die Eide der Beamten und anderer Grossen, wesentlich mit denen zusammen welche die eigentlichen Vassallen bei der Commendation zu schwören hatten, da diese jetzt eben auch auf solche Verhältnisse Anwendung fand."

[27] Guilhiermoz, pp. 127–129: "Les Carolingiens virent dans l'hommage vassalique un moyen si heureux de s'attacher par des liens étroits et de forme humiliante tous ceux dont la puissance pouvait leur porter ombrage qu'ils en firent un des procédés favoris de leur politique. Ils l'imposèrent, et cela dès le règne de Pépin, aux princes étrangers ou quasi indépendants qui se soumettaient de gré ou de force à leur domination, ou qui, déposédés, venaient implorer leur secours. Ils se le firent prêter, d'une façon générale, par tous les grands de royaume, y compris les membres de leur famille, et notamment leurs propres fils." With the exception of the texts with reference to Tassilo (p. 127, n. 9) and to the sons of Louis the Pious (p. 129, n. 12) none of his citations for the ninth century actually call these men *vassals*. These two cases are discussed at length below.

[28] *Ibid.*, p. 130: "Chez les comtes et les personnages de plus haut rang, le caractère vassalique n'était toutefois qu'accessoire et surajouté." Of the three texts which Guilhiermoz cites, p. 130, n. 1, to support this statement, two are from the mid-tenth century, too late to be considered applicable to the Carolingian period; one refers to *quodam fideli vassallo comitique dilecto* and the other to a *comes atque miles*. His third text is taken from Thegan's *Vita Hludowici Imp.*, c. 12. Bernard of Italy is commending himself to his uncle Louis the Pious. According to Thegan, Bernard "tradidit semetipsum ei *ad procerem*." Guilhiermoz italicized the *ad procerem* and added "pour éviter de dire 'ad vassallum'." He failed to give his reasons for this remark, and indeed there seem to be none. In any event it hardly proves that the *caractère vassalique* is *accessoire* and *surajouté*.

[29] *Ibid.*, p. 130: "[Les comtes et les personnages de plus haut rang] ne se confondaient nullement avec les vassaux royaux proprement dits, ceux pour qui ce titre, loin d'être une diminution, était un honneur, et un honneur qui leur procuraient les avantages considérables."

[30] Heinrich Mitteis, *Lehnrecht und Staatsgewalt* (Weimar, 1933), p. 16: "Als Vassus erscheint derjenige, der sich einem Senior in obsequium kommendiert hat. Vasallität und Kommendation in der typischen Form des Einlegens der Hände in die umschliessenden Hände des Seniors gehören von Anfang an zusammen."

[31] *Ibid.*, p. 71.
[32] *Ibid.*, p. 70.
[33] *Ibid.*, pp. 73–75.

[34] *Ibid.*, p. 198: "Zunächst hätte der Ausgangspunkt in der Vasallität liegen können, dergestalt also, dass alle Beamten zwangsläufig zu Vasallen

des Königs geworden, der Amsteid in den Lehnseid verwandelt worden wäre. Etwas Derartiges ist in der Literatur gelegentlich angedeutet, aber, soviel ich sehe, nirgends mit voller Sicherheit behauptet worden. In der Tat wird der Beweis für einen Satz des positiven Rechtes, dass alle Beamten ausnahmslos als solche zur vasallitischen Huldigung verpflichtet gewesen seien, nach Lage der Quellen nicht zu erbringen sein. Aus der vielfach begegnenden Übertragung von Amtsfunktionen an Vasallen kann man darauf um so weniger schliessen, als regelmässig die Kategorie der Vasallen getrennt von der der Beamten angeführt wird. Aus dem vasallitischen obsequium folgt die Pflicht, sich amtlichen Funktionen zu unterziehen, nicht aber zugleich aus dem Beamtendienst die Pflicht zur Huldigung."

[35] And to that extent the vassals are officials; *ibid.*, p. 199, n. 86. Why distinguish then between vassals and *the* officials?

[36] Fustel de Coulanges, *Transformations*, p. 610: "Quant aux comtes, ils étaient avant tout des fonctionnaires royaux; mais ils avaient en même temps un autre caractère. Ces hommes avaient toujours commencé leur carrière par le service du Palais ou ce qu'on appelait la milice palatine; or, pour entrer dans cette milice, il avait fallu se recommander au prince et se faire son fidèle. Ils ne renonçaient assurément pas à cette fidélité le jour où le même prince leur confiait un comté. Ils s'y regardaient plutôt comme des vassaux et des bénéficiaires que comme des représentants de l'autorité publique. Toutes ces idées se confondaient d'ailleurs à tel point que dans le langage du temps un comté était reputé un bénéfice. Dès que ces comtes étaient *des vassaux par rapport* au prince, il était naturel qu'ils eussent eux-mêmes des vassaux."

[37] *Ibid.*, p. 609: "[The Carolingian bishop] 'se recommandait' au roi et lui recommandait en même temps son église, c'est-à-dire tous les hommes qui dépendaient de lui. Cet hommage était de même nature, à peu de chose près, que celui que prêtaient les bénéficiares laïques. Le contrat était conçu dans les mêmes termes et produisait à peu près les mêmes effets."

[38] *Ibid.*, p. 609: "Cet évêque *qui était un vassal* du prince était en même temps un chef de vassaux."

[39] P. Imbart de la Tour, *Les élections épiscopales dans l'église de France du IXe au XIIe siècle* (Paris, 1891), p. 115. ". . . dans tous les cas, la distinction qui peut exister entre l'obligation de l'évêque et celle du *vassus* est si mince, que les textes ne la font pas, et quelle ne peut se conclure d'une analyse minutieuse des documents."

[40] *Ibid.*, p. 116: "Cette conception n'a rien qui doive surprendre, si on se rappelle que l'évêque est un fonctionnaire de même que le comte, et qu'à la fin du IXe siècle tout 'honneur' concédé oblige celui qui l'a reçu à une dépendance spéciale, et que le *vassaticum* devient la forme ordinaire de l'obéissance et de la fidélité."

[41] In Appendix II there are given additional examples of the ambiguities which have arisen in attempts to define Carolingian vassalage.

NOTES 117

CHAPTER II

[42] *Capitularia* (Boretius), I, 336, c. 8: "inter episcopo seu reliquis sacerdotibus, et comitibus et vassis et reliquis fidelibus nostris."

[43] The meaning of *fideles* will be discussed in Chapter III.

[44] *Annales Bertiniani*, anno 837 (ed. G. Waitz, Hannover, 1883, p. 15; in *Scriptores Rerum Germanicarum in Usum Scholarum*): "episcopi, abbates, comites, et vassalli dominici."

[45] *Annales Bertiniani*, anno 877 (Waitz, p. 138); *Capitularia* (Krause), II, 364: "episcopi . . . abbates autem et regni primores ac vassalli regii."

[46] *Capitularia* (Krause), II, 354: "Episcopi, abbates, comites ac vassi dominici ex suis honoribus de unoquoque manso indominicato donent denarios 12, de manso ingenuili etc. . . ."

[47] *Capitularia* (Boretius), I, 298, c. 2: "per mansiones episcoporum et abbatum et comitum qui actores non sunt et vassorum nostrorum."

[48] *Vita Hludowici Imperatoris*, c. 64 (*SS*, II, 648): "Drogo frater imperatoris et episcopus Mettensis, cum aliis episcopis, abbatibus, comitibus, vassis dominicis, plurimaque frequentia tam cleri quam populi."

[49] *Annales Bertiniani*, anno 870 (Waitz, p. 110): "unusquisque eorum [Charles and Louis] 4 episcopos et 10 consiliarios et inter ministeriales et vassallos 30 tantummodo ad idem colloquium ducerent."

[50] See Waitz, III, 529–530; Brunner, II, 107.

[51] *MGH, Diplomata Regum Germaniae ex Stirpe Karolinorum*, II, 52: "in . . . civitate Sena . . . ubi domnus Karolus piissimus imperator in iudicio residebat, adessent cum [eo] Berengerius marchio, item Berengerius, Uualfredus, Bertaldus, Uuinigisus, Gotfredus, Adelbertus, Maurinus et Erardus comitibus [sic], Liuto, Maginfredus, Amilbertus, Ribaldus, Zotem et Berardus vassi idem augusti, Petrus, Fulbertus et Ursepertus iudices sacri palacii, Farulfus comes domni apostolici, et reliqui multis."

[52] Capitulary ascribed to Charlemagne; *Capitularia* (Boretius), I, 213, c. 3: "Ut missi nostri una cum sociis qui in eorum scara commanere videntur episcopis, abbatibus, comites seu vassi nostri cum omni generalitate si necesse fuerit, ubicumque eis iniunctum fuerit, festinare nullatinus tardent." In 780 (?); *Capitularia* (Boretius), I, 52: "Episcopi et abbates atque abbatissae. . . . Comites . . . vassus dominicus." In 787; *Capitularia* (Boretius), I, 198, c. 4: "De episcopis, abbatibus, comitibus seu vassis dominicis vel reliquis hominibus qui ad palatium veniunt. . . ." In 790–800; *Capitularia* (Boretius), I, 203: "Karolus, gratia Dei rex . . . dilectis comitibus seu iudicibus et vassis nostris, vicariis, centenariis vel omnibus missis nostris et agentibus." In 792 or 786; *Capitularia* (Boretius), I, 66, c. 2: "ab episcopis et abbatis sive comitibus vel bassis regalibus necnon vicedomini, archidiaconibus adque canonicis." In 802; *Capitularia* (Boretius), I, 101, c. 18a: "Ut diligenter inquirant inter episcopis, abbatis sive

comites vel abbatissas atque vassos nostros qualem concordiam et amicitiam ad invicem habeant per singula ministeria. . . ." In 807 (?); *Capitularia* (Boretius), I, 136, c. 3: "comites et vassalli nostri." In 816; *Capitularia* (Boretius), I, 264: "Hi vero qui postea venerunt et se aut comitibus aut vassis nostris aut paribus suis se commendaverunt. . . ." In 818-819; *Capitularia* (Boretius), I, 285, c. 18: "aut comitum aut vassallorum nostrorum." In 823-825; *Capitularia* (Boretius), I, 305, c. 11: "Episcopis iterum, abbatibus et vassis nostris et omnibus fidelibus laicis dicimus, ut comitibus ad iustitias faciendas adiutores sitis." In 826; *Capitularia* (Boretius), I, 310: "cum omnibus episcopis, abbatibus, comitibus ac vassis nostris, advocatis nostris, ac vicedominis abbatissarum," to gather at a May placitum. In 845-850; *Capitularia* (Krause), II, 81, c. 3: "comites et vassi dominici." In 864; *Capitularia* (Krause), II, 316, c. 15: "aut comitum aut vassallorum nostrorum." In 866; *Capitularia* (Krause), II, 96, c. 5: "episcopus, comes aut bassus noster." In 869: *Capitularia* (Krause), II, 332, c. 14: "Et missi nostri cum episcopis et comitibus ac vassis nostris. . . ." In 869; *Capitularia* (Krause), II, 334, c. 5: "Ut episcopi comitibus, missis et vassis nostris, sed et ipsis suis subditis, tam clericis quam laicis, et comitum ac vassallorum nostrorum hominibus paternam benignitatem . . . conservent"; *ibid.*, 335, c. 9: "abbates vel abbatissae aut comites seu vassi nostri aut ceteri laici"; *ibid.*, 336, c. 11: "comites et missi ac vassi nostri et ministeriales regni nostri"; c. 12: "episcopi atque abbates et comites ac vassi nostri et omnes fideles laici." In 869; *Capitularia* (Krause), II, 337, c. 2: "vassalli episcoporum, abbatum et abbatissarum atque comitum et vassorum nostrorum . . . aliquis episcopus, abbas aut abbatissa vel comes ac vassus noster . . ."; c. 3: "episcopi atque abbates, comites ac vassi nostri." In 876; *Capitularia* (Krause), II, 103, c. 12: "Ut episcopi comites et vassos nostros in parroechia eorum manentes paterno amore secundum ecclesiasticum ministerium deligant." In 877; *Capitularia* (Krause), II, 354: "De ecclesiis vero, quas comites et vassalli dominici habent . . . de ecclesiis vero imperatoris et imperatricis et comitum ac vassallorum imperialium." In 877; *Capitularia* (Krause), II, 362, c. 4: "si aliquis episcopus vel abbas aut abbatissa vel comes aut vassallus noster obierit. . . ."

[53] The writers actually quoted include Prudentius of Troyes and Hincmar of Rheims (*Annales Bertiniani*), the anonymous author of the *Vita Hludowici Imp.*, and the unknown composers of the capitularies. See notes 42, 44-49, 52.

[54] *Vita Hludowici Imp.*, c. 3 (*SS*, II, 608): "Ordinavit autem per totam Aquitaniam comites, abbates, necnon alios plurimos quos vassos vulgo vocant." Discussed at greater length below, p. 66.

[55] *Capitularia* (Boretius), I, 291, c. 26: "Ut missi nostri qui vel episcopi vel abbates vel comites sunt, quamdiu prope suum beneficium fuerint, nihil de aliorum coniecto accipiant; postquam vero inde longe recesserint, tunc

NOTES

accipiant secundum quod in suo tractoria continetur. Vassi vero nostri et ministeriales qui missi sunt, ubicumque venerint, coniectum accipiant." Concerning *coniectus* see Brunner, II, 310.

⁵⁶ *Capitularia* (Boretius), I, 291, c. 29: "De dispensa missorum nostrorum, qualiter *unicuique iuxta suam qualitatem* dandum vel accipiendum sit: videlicet episcopo panes quadraginta, friskingas tres, de potu modii tres, porcellus unus, pulli tres, ova quindecim, annona ad caballos modii quatuor. Abbati, comiti atque ministeriali nostro unicuique dentur cottidie panes triginta, friskingas duas, de potu modii duo, porcellum unum, pulli tres, ova quindecim, annona ad caballos modii tres. Vassallo nostro panes decem et septem, friskinga una, porcellus unus, de potu modius unus, pulli duo, ova decem, annona ad caballos modii duo." See also below, p. 39.

⁵⁷ See above, n. 45.

⁵⁸ See above, notes 42, 44–49, 52, 54, 55.

⁵⁹ Fustel de Coulanges, *Les origines du système féodal*, pp. 286–287; Waitz, II, pt. I, 222–223, 259, 305; Brunner, II, 353–354; Lot, *Les destinées de l'empire*, p. 666 and his note 140; F. Dahn, *Die Könige der Germanen*, VII, pt. I (Leipzig, 1894), 209; Bloch, *La société féodale, les liens de dépendance*, pp. 239–240.

⁶⁰ Fustel de Coulanges, *Les origines du système féodal*, p. 287; Brunner, II, p. 354, n. 33. Dahn, *op. cit.*, VII, pt. I, 210.

⁶¹ Brunner, I, 451–452.

⁶² Guilhiermoz, p. 56, n. 24; Brunner, II, 354, n. 34.

⁶³ Guilhiermoz, pp. 322–330.

⁶⁴ Brunner, II, 196.

⁶⁵ See below, n. 84.

⁶⁶ *Capitularia* (Boretius), I, 167, c. 7: "De vassis dominicis qui adhuc intra casam serviunt et tamen beneficia habere noscuntur statutum est, ut quicumque ex eis cum domno imperatore domi remanserint vassallos suos casatos secum non retineant, sed cum comite cuius pagenses sunt ire permittat." In 811.

⁶⁷ An interesting letter of Einhard; *MGH*, *Epistolae*, V, 141, No. 63: "Domino sancto et merito venerabili N. summi Dei sacerdoti E[inhartus] p[eccator]. Vassallus iste nomine [Agan]theo propinquus meus est et fuit per aliquantum tempus in meo servitio; sed quia nunc desiderat sub vestro dominatu dies suos ducere, placuit parvitati meae, quod in tam familiari loco esse elegisset, et ideo has commendatorias litteras ei dare decrevi; ut per meam interventionem faciliorem accessum ad vestrum sanctitatem haberet et apud vos resedisset, quem mihi propinquum adsevero. Precor igitur, ut eum suscipere et per servitium vestrum nutrire dignemini. Puto, quod non in[utilem in illo serv]itorem habere debeatis. Opto, ut semper bene valeatis in Domino."

⁶⁸ *Capitularia* (Krause), II, 282, c. 13: "Et mandat vobis [fidelibus]

noster senior [Charles] quia si aliquis de vobis talis est, cui suus senioratus non placet, et illi simulat, ut ad alium seniorem melius quam ad illum acaptare possit, veniat ad illum, et ipse tranquillo et pacifico animo donat illi commeatum; tantum ut ipsi et in suo regno vel suis fidelibus aliquod damnum aut aliquam marritionem non faciat; et quod Deus illi cupierit et ad alium seniorem acaptare potuerit, pacifice habeat."

[69] *Charta Ludovici Pii, HF*, VI, 652: "Omnibus episcopis, abbatibus, abbatissis, comitibus, vicariis, centenariis, seu reliquis fidelibus nostris; notum sit vobis quia istos vassallos nostros, illos et illos, mittimus ad has partes in fiscum promovendas, et varias redibitiones exigendas."

[70] See above, n. 56.

[71] Roth declared that vassals were *Beamten* who had a special function; *Feudalität*, p. 214: "Jedenfalls ergiebt sich daraus ganz zweifellos, dass bei jedem Vassus eine gewisse amtliche Stellung vorausgesetzt wird." They were thus to be distinguished from bishops, abbots, and counts. But he was led into difficulties by an unsuccessful effort to disentangle vassalage and commendation. Bishops, abbots, counts, and *primores* commend themselves and swear fidelity to the king, yet one cannot assert that they became vassals. To solve this problem Roth invented a fallacious theory that these men did not really commend themselves at all; what these men did was to swear at the accession of a new king the oath which holders of benefices had personally to swear to receive back their benefices. Roth, *Geschichte des Beneficialwesens*, p. 385: 'Ursprünglich bildeten also die Vassi dominici gerade wie die Antrustionen eine eigne Classe von Leuten, bey welchen zur Verpflichtung also Unterthanen noch das besondere Dienstverhältniss zum König getreten war. Doch wurde diess schon im neunten Jahrhundert auch auf andere Personen ausgedehnt, und damit der spätere Zustand angebahnt. Es wurde nämlich gewöhnlich, dass die Besitzer von Beneficien sich dem König commendirten, d. h. ihm persönlich den Treueneid leisteten, ohne dass man behaupten könnte, dass sie Vassallen geworden seyen; es wäre wenigstens sonst nicht erklärlich, dass solche Beneficiare, Bischöfe, Aebte, Grafen und Primores, von den Vasalli dominici ausdrücklich unterschieden werden. Die äussere Veranlassung dazu lag wohl darin, dass beim Thronfall der Beneficiar die Erneuerung des Beneficiums persönlich nachsuchen musste, und dass damit die unmittelbare Ableistung des Fidelitätseides in die Hände des Königs von selbst in Verbindung trat." Repeated in his *Feudalität*, pp. 276-278. This theory did not survive the attack of Waitz, "Über die Anfänge der Vassallität," *Gesammelte Abhandlungen* (Gottingen, 1896), p. 25; and it carried with itself to an undeserved grave, or at least to Limbo, Roth's valuable assertion that vassals were functionaries distinct from bishops, abbots, and counts and that therefore the latter were not vassals. The fallacious theory with which Roth tried to bolster up this assertion explains in part its demise. Another reason is that Roth did not

succeed in identifying the characteristics which mark vassals off from bishops, counts, and abbots and so explain this distinction; see *Feudalität*, pp. 214–216. It will be remembered, also, that a number of historians had difficulty in distinguishing between office in general and vassalage.

[72] Such a conclusion may not appear surprising at first, but I call special attention to the fact that a vassal is just that *and no more*: he is not a bishop or count, and vice versa, a bishop or a count is not a vassal. The military character of vassalage has of course impressed itself upon earlier writers. It is especially noticeable in Guilhiermoz (p. 56) and Brunner (II, 349–368 *passim*), and yet they considered men other than "real" vassals as vassals for the reason that they were *commendati*. They had not reconciled their warrior vassal with those other men whom they called vassals. Dopsch gave an excellent translation of *vassus* as *Berufskrieger* (*Wirtschaftsentwicklung der Karolingerzeit* [2nd ed.], II, 22 and *Grundlagen der europ. Kulturentwicklung*, II, 139), yet because he identified commendation with vassalage, he devised a theory that clerics and women gave fidelity and service which is somehow or other not commendation. The reason for this is clear: to escape the conclusion that clerics and women are vassals, i. e., warriors. In a later article ("Beneficialwesen und Feudalität," *Mitteilungen des Österreichischen Instituts für Geschichtsforschung*, XLVI [1932], 19) Dopsch does not emphasize so much the military character of the vassals; after observing that vassals are found performing financial, judicial, and administrative services, he says: "Es war keineswegs nur der Reiterdienst, der das Anschwellen der Vasallität verursachte, noch liegt m. E. sowohl der rechtsgeschichtliche als der politische Schwerpunkt der Vasallität in der kriegerischen Dienstpflicht der Vasallen, mindestens nicht in der Karolingerzeit." The reasons for insisting, contrary to Dopsch, that the most important tasks of the vassals were military and police work will be evident in the following pages. Imbart de la Tour (*Les élections épiscopales*, pp. 115–116) says that if bishops, abbots, counts, and vassals are distinguished in the texts as Roth had said, it is not because their relations with the king are different but because their functions are different. With that there can be no quarrel. But then he adds that the texts do not show any differences in the obligations of bishops and vassals and that between bishops and kings there is the bond of vassalage. What does it mean then to be a vassal? Richard Schroeder and Eberhard von Kunssberg (*Lehrbuch der deutschen Rechtsgeschichte* [7th ed., Berlin and Leipzig, 1932], pp. 168–171) describe vassals as men who serve their seignior as "kriegerisches Gefolge"; their references to commendation (see their index) are so brief that the relationships between commendation, vassals, and other servants are not made clear. They apparently regard *homo, fidelis, vassus*, as all one and the same; *op. cit.*, p. 168. Bloch also emphasizes the military character of vassalage; see below, pp. 143, 144. Likewise, F. L.

Ganshof, "Benefice and Vassalage," *Cambridge Historical Journal*, VI (1939), 166, 168–169.

[73] *Opusculum LV Capitulorum Adversus Hincmarum Laudunensem*, Migne, *PL*, t. 126, col. 491B: ". . . multi te apud plurimos dicunt de fortitudine et agilitate tui corporis gloriari, et de praeliis, atque ut nostratium lingua dicitur, de *vassaticis* frequenter ac libenter sermonem habere, et qualiter ageres si laicus fuisses irreverentur referre, et alia multa quae tibi non conveniunt dicere et agere, nec mihi enuntiare." This letter, written in the spring or summer of 870, is No. 282 in the register drawn up by Heinrich Schrörs, *Hinkmar Erzbischof von Reims* (Freiburg-im-Breisgau, 1884).

[74] *Concilium Germanicum* held by Carloman, son of Charles Martel, April 21, 742, a reforming council under the influence of St. Boniface, see Charles Joseph Hefele, *Histoire des conciles* (tr. and ed. by H. Leclercq), III² (1910), 815; *Capitularia* (Boretius), I, 25, c. 2; *MGH, Concilia* (Werminghoff), II, 3, c. 2: "Servis Dei per omnia omnibus armaturam portare vel pugnare aut in exercitum et in hostem pergere omnino prohibuimus, nisi illi tantummodo, qui propter divinum ministerium, missarum scilicet solemnia adinplenda et sanctorum patrocinia portanda, ad hoc electi sunt; id est unum vel duos episcopos cum capellanis presbiteris princeps secum habeat, et unusquisque praefectus unum presbiterum, qui hominibus peccata confitentibus iudicare et indicare poenitentiam possint." Provincial synod of Riesbach in 798 (?); *MGH, Concilia* (Werminghoff), II, 197, c. 1: "Ut nullus clericus vestimenta laicalia portet nec arma; nisi tantum, quod ipsius religioni deceat, induere praesumat." *Capitula a sacerdotibus proposita* in 802; *Capitularia* (Boretius), I, 107, c. 18: "Nemo ex sacerdotum numero arma pugnantium umquam portet nec litem contra proximum ullam excitet." *Concilium Moguntinense* in 813; *MGH, Concilia* (Werminghoff), II, 266: "De armis dimittendis. XVII. Nos autem, qui saeculum relinquimus, id modis omnibus observare volumus, ut arma spiritalia habeamus, saecularia dimittamus. Laicis vero, qui apud nos sunt, arma portare non praeiudicemus, quia antiquus mos est et ad nos usque pervenit." Council of Meaux and Paris in 845; *Capitularia* (Krause), II, 407, c. 37: "Ut, quicumque ex clero esse videntur, arma militaria non sumant nec armati incedant, sed professionis suae vocabulum religiosis moribus et religioso habitu praebeant. Quodsi contempserint, tamquam sacrorum canonum contemptores et ecclesiasticae sanctitatis profanitores proprii gradus amissione multentur, quia non possunt simul Deo et saeculo militare." Charles the Bald's capitulary of Pavia, February, 876 *Capitularia* (Krause), II, 102, c. 9: ". . . Venationem quoque nullus tam sacri ordinis exercere praesumat neque arma militaria pro qualicumque seditione portare audeat aut habitum quemlibet tantum apicem sacerdotum non decentem assumat." This was reissued at the council held at Ponthion in June, 876; Mansi, XVIIᴬ, col. 312.

[75] Note that *fortitudo*, a characteristic of vassals, is one of the things in which Hincmar of Laon takes pride; see above, n. 73.

[76] *Vita Hludowici Imp.*, c. 3 (*SS*, II, 608): "[Charlemagne] ordinavit autem per totam Aquitaniam comites, abbates, necnon alios plurimos quos vassos vulgo vocant, ex gente Francorum, quorum prudentiae et fortitudini nulli calliditate nulli vi obviare fuerit tutum, eisque commisit curam regni prout utile iudicavit, finium tutamen, villarumque regiarum ruralem provisionem." The relative clause *quos vassos vulgo etc.* refers not to the counts and abbots but only to the *alios plurimos*; discussed at length below, pp. 66 ff.

[77] *Capitulare Bononiense* of 811; *Capitularia* (Boretius), I, 167, c. 10: "Constitutum est, ut nullus episcopus aut abbas aut abbatissa vel quislibet rector aut custos aecclesiae bruniam vel gladium sine nostro permisso cuilibet homini extraneo aut dare aut venundare praesumat, nisi tantum vassallis suis."

It was probably of Abbot Fulrad's vassals that Charlemagne was thinking when he ordered him to appear with his men well armed and prepared for a military expedition; in a letter of 804-811 Charlemagne announces to Fulrad that there is to be a *placitum* at Strassfurt; *Capitularia* (Boretius), I, 168: "Quapropter precipimus tibi, ut pleniter cum hominibus tuis bene armatis ac preparatis ad predictum locum venire debeas XV Kal. Jul. quod est septem diebus ante missam sancti Johannis baptiste. Ita vero preparatus cum hominibus tuis ad predictum locum venies, ut inde, in quamcumque partem nostra fuerit iussio; et exercitaliter ire possis; id est cum armis, etc. . . ."

[78] *Capitularia* (Boretius), I, 67, c. 4: ". . . adque servi, qui honorati beneficia et ministeria tenent vel in bassallatico honorati sunt cum domini sui et caballos, arma et scuto et lancea spata et senespasio habere possunt: omnes iurent" the oath of fidelity to the king (792 or 786). It is clear why the king had even these unfree men swear fidelity to him; those who acted as functionaries and were endowed with benefices were influential, and those who acted as vassals represented a military danger if their loyalty were questionable.

[79] *Capitularia* (Krause), II, 86, c. 1: ". . . ut comites nostri eorumque sculdassi, adjunctis secum vassallis episcoporum, si necessitas fuerit, ubicumque tales [bandits] audierint, studiosissime perquirant et eos capiant atque distringant." End of 850.

[80] *Capitularia* (Boretius), I, 300, c. 4: "De vassis nostris qui ad marcam nostram constituti sunt custodiendam. . . ." In 821.

[81] See above, n. 76.

[82] See below, n. 235.

[83] *Capitularia* (Krause), II, 96, c. 4: "Quodsi comes aut bassi nostri aliqua infirmitate [non] detenti remanserint, aut abbates vel abbatissae si

plenissime homines suos non direxerint, ipsi suos honores perdant, et eorum bassalli et proprium et beneficium amittant. De episcopis autem cuiuscumque bassallus remanserit, et proprium et beneficium perdant."

[84] *Capitularia* (Boretius), I, 291, c. 27: "Ut vassi nostri et vassi episcoporum, abbatum, abbatissarum et comitum, qui anno praesente in hoste non fuerunt, heribannum rewadient; exceptis his qui propter necessarias causas et a domno ac genitore nostro Karolo constitutas domi dimissi fuerunt; id est qui a comite propter pacem conservandam et propter coniugem ac domum eius custodiendam, et ab episcopo vel abbate vel abbatissa similiter propter pacem conservandam et propter fruges colligendas et familiam constringendam et missos recipiendos dimissi fuerunt."

[85] Perhaps in chasing bandits as in n. 79 above.

[86] Notice the royal vassals performing a similar task for the king, above, n. 69.

[87] *Walafridi Strabonis Libellus de Exordiis et Incrementis Quarundam in Observationibus Ecclesiasticis Rerum* (*Capitularia*, [Krause], II, 515): "Sicut augusti Romanorum totius orbis monarchiam tenuisse feruntur, ita summus pontifex in sede Romana vicem beati Petri gerens totius ecclesiae apice sublimatur. . . . Deinde archiepiscopos . . . regibus conferamus; metropolitanos autem ducibus comparemus. . . . Quod comites vel praefecti in saeculo, hoc episcopi ceteri in ecclesia explent. . . . Quemadmodum sunt in palatiis praetores vel comites palatii, qui saecularium causas ventilant, ita sunt et illi, quos summos cappellanos Franci appellant, clericorum causis praelati. Cappellani minores ita sunt, sicut hi, quos vassos dominicos Gallica consuetudine nominamus. Dicti sunt autem primitus cappellani a cappa beati Martini, quam reges Francorum ob adiutorium victoriae in proeliis solebant secum habere, quam ferentes et custodientes cum ceteris sanctorum reliquiis clerici cappellani coeperunt vocari." Written between 840 and 842; see *Capitularia* (Krause), II, 473.

[88] *Monachus Sangallensis*, lib. I, c. 11 (*SS*, II, 736): "Comedente autem Karolo, ministrabant duces et tiranni, vel reges diversarum gentium. Post cuius convivium cum illi comederent, serviebant eis comites et praefecti, vel diversarum dignitatum proceres. Ipsis quoque manducandi finem facientibus, militares viri vel scolares aulae reficiebantur. Post hos omnimodorum officiorum magistri, deinde ministri, post inde vero eorundem ministrorum ministri, ita ut ultimi ante noctis medium non manducarent." This was actually written long after Charlemagne's death, *circa* 883–887; see Louis Halphen, *Études critiques sur l'histoire de Charlemagne* (Paris, 1921), pp. 112–113. It is probable that the description given here applies not to the *palatium* of Charlemagne but to that of contemporaries of the monk; still, in such matters there may well have been a time-honored custom. It accords well with the inferior position of the vassal, already noted above, pp. 25–27.

[89] See above, n. 56.

NOTES 125

⁹⁰ Édouard Beaudouin, "La recommendation et la justice seigneuriale," *Annales de l'enseignement supérieur de Grenoble*, I (1889), 52-54, asserted that the vassal of a private seignior had no military obligation toward his seignior; that the vassal owed military service only to the king though he might be led to the army by his seignior, a reiteration of Waitz, IV, 276. If this were true, one might well wonder why these men who did not render military service to their lords were called vassals; or since they were so called, if the term vassal really meant armed servant. But Brunner, II, 360-361, observed that he who professes this theory "bemüht sich vergebens, die Ausbildung und Verbreitung der ganzen Institution zu erklären." It is true that Charlemagne in the *Capitulare Haristallense* of 779 forbade anyone to have a troop of armed men; *Capitularia* (Boretius), I, 50, c. 14: "De truste faciendo nemo praesumat." But this did not establish any permanent policy, for Charlemagne himself later ordered that unfree men who, honored by their lords with vassalage, had been given horses and arms should promise to him an oath of fidelity; see above n. 78. He did not forbid the arming of these men. In 811 he ordered that bishops, abbots, and abbesses should not give arms to anyone *save their vassals*; see above, n. 77. As Esmein, *Cours*, p. 117, has remarked, even if private wars were forbidden, they were not a rare occurrence and vassals certainly had to defend their lords. Lot, *Les destinées de l'empire*, p. 659, says that if the vassals of private lords were not to be used in private wars for their seigniors but were to fight only in the king's army, still they were armed guards who defended their lords against enemies and brigands. And we must recognize these latter men as regular occupants of the Frankish empire. Private seigniors did have in their service men who protected them arms in hand, men who could well be named vassals. The king, finally recognizing the existence of these armed men in the service of private seigniors, ordered their seigniors to lead them to the royal army when it assembled at the beginning of a campaign; he also made use of them on occasion in policing the realm; see above, n. 79.

⁹¹ Waitz, IV, 533-534; Fustel de Coulanges, *Transformations*, p. 511.
⁹² Brunner, II, 269-271.
⁹³ Waitz, IV, 537-538, 574, 581; Brunner, II, 288, n. 78.
⁹⁴ Fustel de Coulanges, *Transformations*, p. 513.
⁹⁵ Waitz, IV, 539-540; Brunner, II, 273, n. 10.
⁹⁶ Waitz, IV, 552-553.
⁹⁷ Waitz, IV, 539-540.
⁹⁸ Waitz, IV, 541-542; Fustel de Coulanges, *Transformations*, p. 514.
⁹⁹ Waitz, IV, 554; Brunner, II, 273.
¹⁰⁰ Waitz, IV, 554-574; Brunner, II, 272-276.
¹⁰¹ Waitz, IV, 542-547; Brunner, II, 277-281; F. Lot, *Les destinées de l'empire*, p. 558.
¹⁰² *Capitularia* (Krause), II, 321, c. 26: "Ut pagenses Franci, qui ca-

ballos habent vel habere possunt, cum suis comitibus in hostem pergant."
[103] *Annales Fuldenses*, anno 891 (ed. F. Kurze, Hannover, 1891, p. 120; in *Scriptores Rerum Germanicarum in Usum Scholarum*): "quia Francis pedetemptim certare inusitatum est."
[104] Bloch, *La société féodale, les liens de dépendance*, pp. 234–237.
[105] Brunner, II, 277–279.
[106] Letter of Louis the Pious and his son Lothair in 828; *Capitularia* (Krause), II, 5: "iubemus ut omnes homines per totum regnum nostrum, qui exercitalis itineris debitores sunt, bene sint praeparati cum equis, armis, vestimentis, carris et victualibus; ut, quocumque tempore eis a nobis denuntiatum fuerit, sine ulla mora exire et, in quamcumque partem necessitas postulaverit, pergere possint et tamdiu ibi esse, quamdiu necessitas postulaverit."
[107] Lot, *Les destinées de l'empire*, pp. 657–663.
[108] Childbert gave the Bavarians a duke, in the person of Tassilo I in 595; Lot, *Les destinées de l'empire*, p. 273.
[109] Waitz, II, pt. II, 366–372; Brunner, II, 213–214.
[110] Brunner, II, 56.
[111] H. Hahn, *Jahrbücher des fränkischen Reichs, 741–752* (Berlin, 1863), pp. 43–49; Lot, *op. cit.*, p. 403.
[112] Born in 742; L. Oelsner, *Jahrbücher des fränkischen Reichs unter König Pippin* (Leipzig, 1871), p. 264.
[113] Hahn, *op. cit.*, pp. 115–117; Waitz, III, 46; Lot, *op. cit.*, p. 405.
[114] See Lot, *op. cit.*, p. 405, n. 69.
[115] Waitz, III, 46, n. 4.
[116] *Ibid.*, n. 3.
[117] Oelsner, *op. cit.*, p. 296.
[118] Oelsner, *op. cit.*, pp. 264, 302–303.
[119] *Annales Regni Francorum*, anno 757 (ed. F. Kurze, Hannover, 1895, p. 14; in *Scriptores Rerum Germanicarum in Usum Scholarum*): "Et rex Pippinus tenuit placitum suum in Compendio cum Francis; ibique Tassilo venit, dux Baioariorum, in vassatico se commendans per manus, sacramenta iuravit multa et innumerabilia, reliquias sanctorum manus imponens, et fidelitatem promisit regi Pippino et supradictis filiis eius, domno Carolo et Carlomanno, sicut vassus recta mente et firma devotione per iustitiam, sicut vassus dominos suos esse deberet. Sic confirmavit supradictus Tassilo supra corpus sancti Dionisii, Rustici et Eleutherii necnon et sancti Germani seu sancti Martini, ut omnibus diebus vitae eius sic conservaret, sicut sacramentis promiserat; sic et eius homines maiores natu, qui erant cum eo, firmaverunt, sicut dictum est, in locis superius nominatis quam et in aliis multis."
[120] F. Lot, "Le serment de fidélité," *Rev. belge de philol. et d'hist.*, XII (1933), 576.

NOTES 127

[121] A. Dumas, "Le serment de fidélité," *Rev. belge de philol. et d'hist.*, XIV (1935), 418-419.

[122] Notice the last clause in the statement of the *Annales Regni Francorum*, quoted above, n. 119.

[123] For *vassus* applied to Witzin and to the sons of Louis the Pious see below, pp. 60, 68.

[124] Three times; *Annales Regni Francorum* (Kurze), pp. 14, 15, 78.

[125] With reference to unfree men honored by their masters with vassalage who are required to swear the oath of fidelity to the king; see above, n. 78. In the same capitulary the *missi* are ordered to report the number and names of those who have sworn fidelity; the counts shall also report concerning those who were born within the *pagus* and were *pagensales* and concerning those who have commended themselves in vassalage to anyone. The king presumably wants to know something of the number of trained and equipped soldiers in the kingdom as well as of the actual free population; *Capitularia* (Boretius), I, 67, c. 4: ". . . Et nomina vel numerum de ipsis qui iuraverunt ipsi missi in brebem secum adportent; et comites similiter de singulis centenis semoti, tam de illos qui infra pago nati sunt et pagensales fuerint, quamque et de illis qui aliunde in bassalatico commendati sunt." In another Charlemagne orders that no one is to receive a Lombard into vassalage or into his household before he knows where and in what condition the man was born. Charlemagne is not speaking of great magnates who serve him, but of men who serve his subjects and of men who are thought of in the same breath with one's household; *Capitularia* (Boretius), I, 191, c. 11: "Ut nullus quilibet hominem Langobardiscum in vassatico vel in casa sua recipiat, antequam sciat unde sit vel quomodo natus est." In a capitulary of 787 Pepin, son of Charlemagne, speaks of men who are in the vassalage not of himself but of his subjects; *Capitularia* (Boretius), I, 199, c. 5: "Stetit nobis de illos homines qui hic intra Italia eorum seniores dimittunt, ut nullus eos debeat recipere in vassatico sine commeatu senioris sui, antequam sciat veraciter, pro qua causa aut culpa ipse suum seniorem dimisit." A capitulary of Louis the Pious in 815 which concerns itself with Spaniards who commend themselves *in vassaticum* to the counts; and not to the king, be it noted; *Capitularia* (Boretius), I, 262, c. 6: "Noverint tamen iidem Hispani sibi licentiam a nobis esse concessam, ut se in vassaticum comitibus nostris more solito commendent. . . ." This is repeated by Charles the Bald in 844; *Capitularia* (Krause), II, 260, c. 10. Krause included in his edition of the *Capitularia* the letter of the bishops in 858 to Louis the German which contains the celebrated passage: "We bishops, consecrated to God, are not men of such a kind that we should commend ourselves to anyone in vassalage like secular men"; *ibid.*, 439, l. 32: "Et nos episcopi Domino consecrati non sumus huiusmodi homines, ut, sicut homines saeculares, in vassallatico de-

NOTES

beamus nos cuilibet commendare." We may take their word and not include the bishops among those who commend themselves in vassalage. This passage in the bishops' letter is discussed at length in Appendix III.

[126] Numerous cases; see notes 6, 246, 249, 250, 255, 264, 265, 266, 270, 272, 279, 280, 281, 282, 286, 287.

[127] See below, n. 218.

[128] *Annales Regni Francorum* (Kurze), p. 15: ". . . et more Francico in manus regis in vassaticum manibus suis semetipsum commendavit fidelitatemque tam ipso regi Pippino quam filiis eius Karlo et Carlomanno iureiurando supra corpus sancti Dionysii promisit; et non solum ibi, sed etiam super corpus sancti Martini et sancti Germani simili sacramento fidem se praedictis dominis suis diebus vitae suae servaturum est pollicitus."

[129] Exceptions are the three times with regard to Tassilo (n. 119 and n. 128 above, and below, n. 138), three times in the capitularies and once in the letter of the bishops in 858 (above, n. 125). Seven times, one of which is a repetition, and *three* of which have to do with Tassilo!

[130] See above, n. 119.

[131] *Annales Regni Francorum*, anno 763 (Kurze), pp. 20–23.

[132] Sigurd Abel and Bernhard Simson, *Jahrbücher des fränkischen Reichs unter Karl dem Grossen*, I (Leipzig, 1888), 51–52.

[133] Abel and Simson, *op. cit.*, I, 65.

[134] Lot, *Les destinées de l'empire*, p. 440.

[135] *Annales Regni Francorum*, anno 781 (Kurze, p. 58): "Et tunc missi sunt suo missi ab apostolico supradicto . . . ad Tassilonem ducem una cum missis domni regis Caroli . . . ad commonendum et contestandum, ut reminisceret priscorum sacramentorum suorum et ut non aliter faceret, nisi sicut iureiurando iam dudum promiserat ad partem domni Pippini regis et domni Caroli magni regis vel Francorum. Et tunc consensit Tassilo dux Baioariorum, ut sumptos obsides a domno rege Carolo et tunc ad eius veniret praesentiam. . . . Et coniungens se supradictus dux in praesentiam piissimi regis ad Wormatiam civitatem, ibi renovans sacramenta et dans duodecim obsides electos, ut omnia conservaret, quicquid domno Pippino regi iureiurando promiserat in causa supradicti domni Caroli regis vel fidelium suorum; qui et ipsi obsides recepti sunt in Carisiacum villa de manu Sinberti episcopi. Sed non diu praefatus dux Tassilo promissiones, quas fecerat, conservavit."

[136] Gathered by Abel and Simson, *op. cit.*, I, 396, n. 2.

[137] The texts agree upon the fact that Tassilo went to Charlemagne only under pressure. See the texts gathered in Abel and Simson, *op. cit.*, I, 600, n. 2.

[138] *Annales Regni Francorum*, anno 787 (Kurze, p. 78): "undique constrictus Tassilo venit per semetipsum, tradens se manibus in manibus domni regis Caroli in vassaticum et reddens ducatum sibi commissum a domno

NOTES

Pippino rege, et recredidit se in omnibus peccasse et male egisse. Tunc denuo renovans sacramenta et dedit obsides electos XII et tertium decimum filium suum Theodonem."

[139] Abel and Simson, *op. cit.*, I, 600, n. 6, gives the texts from other annals.

[140] *Annales Regni Francorum*, anno 783 (Kurze, p. 80): "ibique veniens Tassilo ex iussione domni regis, sicut et ceteri eius vassi."

[141] His son Theodo had been given to Charles as a hostage the year before.

[142] *Annales Regni Francorum*, anno 788 (Kurze, p. 80): "et quid magis, confessus est se dixisse, etiamsi decem filios haberet, omnes voluisset perdere, antequam placita sic manerent vel stabile permitteret, sicut iuratum habuit; et etiam dixit, melius se mortuum esse quam ita vivere."

[143] M. Dumas called attention to this text, "tradens se manibus eius ut servus," to prove that *vassaticum* means *servitium*; it does but it means the service of one who is of inferior rank if he can be called *servus*. See Dumas, "Le serment de fidélité," *Rev. belge de philol. et d'hist.*, XIV (1935), 419, n. 2.

[144] Closely contemporary with the commendation of Tassilo in 787 is the capitulary of Charlemagne concerning unfree men who, honored by their masters with vassalage, must swear an oath of fidelity to the king. See above, n. 78.

[145] So unusual that as we have seen Dumas would not translate *vassaticum* itself as vassalage. Krawinkel says that Tassilo's commendation into vassalage was unusual, not typical; see Appendix IV.

[146] Waitz, IV, 282, n. 1.

[147] *Monachus Sangallensis*, II, 10 (*SS*, II, 753): "Quando, inquiens, vester eram vassallus, post vos, ut oportuit, inter commilitones meos steteram; nunc autem, vester socius et commilito, non inmerito me vobis coaequo."

[148] *Monachus Sangallensis*, II, 10 (*SS*, II, 753). Concerning the credulity and talespinning of the monk, see L. Halphen, *Études critiques sur l'histoire de Charlemagne* (Paris, 1921), pp. 104–142.

[149] Waitz, IV, 282, n. 2.

[150] *Monachus Sangallensis*, I, 13 (*SS*, II, 736): "Providentissimus Karolus nulli comitum, nisi his qui in confinio vel termino barbarorum constituti erant, plus quam unum comitatum aliquando concessit, nulli episcoporum abbateiam vel aecclesias ad ius regium pertinentes, nisi ex certissimis causis unquam permisit; cumque a consiliariis sive a familiaribus suis interrogaretur, cur ita faceret, respondit: Cum illo fisco vel curte, illa abbateiola vel aecclesia, tam bonum vel meliorem vassallum, quam ille comes est aut episcopus, fidelem mihi facio."

[151] *Annales Laureshamenses*, anno 802 (*SS*, I, 38): "[domnus Caesar

NOTES

Carolus] recordatus misericordiae suae de pauperibus, qui in regno suo erant et iustitias suas pleniter abere non poterant, noluit de infra palatio pauperiores vassos suos transmittere ad iustitias faciendum propter munera, sed elegit in regno suo archiepiscopos et reliquos episcopos et abbates cum ducibus et comitibus, qui iam opus non abebant super innocentes munera accipere, et ipsos misit per universum regnum suum, ut ecclesiis, viduis et orfanis et pauperibus et cuncto populo iustitiam facerent."

[152] *Annales Laureshamenses*, anno 799 (*SS*, I, 38).

[153] Mitteis, *Lehnrecht und Staatsgewalt*, p. 198, n. 84, says of this text that it "kann auch anders gefasst werden," that is, other than meaning that bishops, priests, and counts are vassals. His views are indicated above, p. 13.

[154] *SS*, II, 608.

[155] *Annales Regni Francorum*, anno 789 (Kurze, p. 84): "Fuerunt cum eo in eodem exercitu Franci, Saxones, Frisiones. . . . Fuerunt etiam Sclavi cum eo, quorum vocabula sunt Suurbi, nec non et Abotriti, quorum princeps fuit Witzan." Copied in the *Annales Fuldenses*, anno 789 (Kurze, p. 11). The other annals do not mention him at this date; see Abel and Simson, *Karl der Grosse*, II, 4, n. 7.

[156] *Annales Laureshamenses*, anno 795 (*SS*, I, 36).

[157] Other texts mentioning Witzin are the one above; n. 155 and those gathered by Abel and Simson, *op. cit.*, II, 95, n. 9. For *Poeta Saxo* see *SS*, I, 251–252.

[158] See above, n. 155.

[159] See n. 157. For a similar inadequacy in terminology see the *Annales Einhardi* for 789 in *Annales Regni Francorum* (Kurze), pp. 85, 87.

[160] See Abel and Simson, *op. cit.*, II, 95.

[161] *Gesta Aldrici*, c. 47, *MGH*, *Concilia* (Werminghoff), II, 837: "Precepit enim hanc justitiam inquirere domnus imperator Ebroino Pictaviensis urbis episcopo et Erchinrado Parisiace civitatis episcopo et Rorigoni comiti et Altmaro seneschalco domne Judith imperatricis et misso palatino una cum aliis vassis dominicis." In or just before 837.

[162] See Guilhiermoz, pp. 130–137; quotation from Dumas given below, notes 380, 381; quotation from Lot given below, n. 383. From such a conclusion Petot does not shrink; see quotation given above, n. 17.

[163] On the seneschal see Brunner, II, 169.

[164] *Concilia* (Werminghoff), II, 847.

[165] Migne, *PL*, t. 115, col. 77–87; *Concilia* (Werminghoff), II, 836–847.

[166] See Julien Havet, *Oeuvres* (Paris, 1896), I, 273.

[167] *Ibid.*, I, 109, article published in 1887.

[168] *Ibid.*, I, 317, in an article unfinished at his death in 1893 and published posthumously among his collected works.

NOTES 131

[169] J. F. Böhmer, *Die Regesten des Kaiserreichs unter den Karolingern* (reworked by E. Mühlbacher, 2nd ed., Innsbruck, 1908), No. 976, p. 395.

[170] *Concilia* (Werminghoff), II, 835.

[171] Bernhard Simson, *Die Entstehung der Pseudo-Isidorischen Fälschungen in Le Mans* (Leipzig, 1886), p. 127: "hochst freigebig." See also Bernhard Simson, *Jahrbücher des fränkischen Reichs unter Ludwig dem Frommen* (Leipzig, 1874–1876), II, 243; and Böhmer-Mühlbacher, *op. cit.*, No. 976, p. 396.

[172] Waitz, III, 530, n. 1.

[173] Waitz, IV, 242, n. 5; text in Trudpertus Neugart, *Codex Diplomaticus Alemanniae et Burgundiae Trans-Juranae* (Typis San-Blasianis, 1791), I, 329. It is No. 1222 of Böhmer-Mühlbacher, *Regesten*; Pepin, a layman, was not only a count but also an abbot; *Annales Bertiniani*, anno 858 (Waitz, p. 50): "Cum quo Pippinum iam laicum venientem suscipit et ei comitatus ac monasteria in Aquitania tribuit." Monasteries were not infrequently given to laymen; see *Annales Bertiniani*, anno 859 (Waitz, p. 51): "Karlus quaedam monasteria, quae antea clerici habere solebant, laicis distribuit."

[174] *Vita Walae*, II, c. 17 (*SS*, II, 563; Radbert's *Epitaphium Arsenii*, edited by Ernst Dümmler in *Abhandlung der Königlichen Akademie der Wissenschaften zu Berlin*, 1899–1900, p. 85): "Tamen ut elucescant quae proposui, commemoranda sunt capitula, quae augustus pater quasi pro querela filiis direxit, ut enuntiaret quid contra requireret.

"Primum rememorari eos monet, quod filii eius sint, et ipse eos Deo auctore genuerit.

"Ad quod ipsi: 'Gratias omnipotenti Deo, inquiunt, qui quod verum est de nobis, talia recogitare vobis concessit, et quia non solum recogitare, verum etiam mandare dignati estis. Nos enim, precellentissime augustorum, in vita nihil post Deum carius habemus, quam vos sacratissimum genitorem; nihil gloriosius possidemus, quam quia vestri filii censemur et sumus; nihil locupletius, nihil ditius, nihilque nobis magnificentius ad honores, ad excellentiam et dignitatem, ad laudem nominis et splendorem gloriae. Idcirco, gloriosissime, venimus humiles et devoti, subditi, ut decet, et subiecti, tantum dignetur pietas vestra et mansuetudo recogitare de nobis, ne condemnemur iniuste, ne abdicemur sine crimine, ne exheredemur sine culpa. Non enim insurgimus contra vos, sicut locuntur et accusant nos, qui nos perdere inimici moliuntur, sed supplices veniam, indulgentiam et misericordiam postulamus.'

"Deinde in alio capitulo: 'Mementote, inquit, etiam et quod mei vasalli estis, mihique cum iuramento fidem firmastis.'

"Ad quod rursus iidem: 'Bene, inquiunt, recolimus ita esse uti mandastis, quoniam et a natura, et a promissis, et ab omni verae fidei sacramento profecto fideles sumus. Unde sicut numquam deseruimus militiae vestrae servitutem, ita donec spiritus in nobis superest, numquam desertores erimus, quia nobis gloria vestra, honor et prosperitas carior est, quam vita nostra, etc.'" For the remainder of their long-winded lying see *op. cit.*

[175] For *fides* as the responsibility to serve another as well as to be faithful, see below, n. 220.

[176] It will be remembered that according to the Monk of St. Gall Louis the German renounced his vassalage to his father at the age of six.

[177] Bernhard Simson, *Jahrbücher des fränkischen Reichs unter Ludwig dem Frommen*, II, 38–39.

[178] *Eph.* 6, 1.

[179] *Eph.* 6, 4.

[180] *Vita Walae*, II, c. 17 (*SS*, II, 563; Dümmler, *Epitaphium*, p. 85): "Propterea ex lege Dei, non minus quam ex lege patriae, de istis colligendus est modus iustitiae, etiam ex lege nature, quia, sicut scriptum est, *filii oboedite* vel deferte *parentibus*, ita et *patres nolite ad iracundiam provocare filios vestros*. Quod si utrumque servatum providenter esset, tantum malum non adcrevisset. Tamen ut elucescant, *etc.*" as in n. 174.

[181] This is a portion of the second book which was composed at the very earliest in 852; see Dümmler, *Epitaphium*, p. 11.

[182] In *Die Vitae Walae* cited by Dümmler, *Epitaphium*, p. 15, n. 1.

[183] *Ibid.*, p. 15, n. 1.

[184] *Ibid.*, p. 15.

[185] See note 174 *in fine*.

[186] See above, p. 27.

[187] In a diploma of Louis the Pious, cited by Waitz, III, 506, n. 5: "Agbertus comes et ostiarius atque consiliarius noster."

[188] The texts which permit a broad interpretation do not date from any one point within the period under consideration here (752–888). They are dated as follows: *Annales Regni Francorum*, about 788; see *Annales Regni Francorum*, ed. Kurze, p. VI. The *Annales Laureshamenses* stop with the year 806. The *Gesta Aldrici* was written shortly before June, 840; see A. Molinier, *Les sources de l'histoire de France*, I (Paris, 1901), No. 821. The *Vita Hludowici Pii* was written shortly after 840; see Molinier, *op. cit.*, I, No. 749. The *Vita Walae* dates from about 852; see n. 181 above. The Monk of St. Gall wrote his life of Charlemagne between 884–887; see Molinier, *op. cit.*, I, No. 650.

[189] For *vassi dominici* see notes 46, 48, 52, 66, 242, 246; *vassalli regii*, n. 250; *vassalli imperiales*, n. 52; *vassi augusti*, n. 51.

[190] See above n. 84.

[191] Capitulary of Pitres in 869, *Capitularia* (Krause), II, 336, c. 11: "Ut comites et missi ac vassi nostri et ministeriales regni nostri unusquisque secundum ordinem et dignitatem ac possibilitatem suam pacem et iustitiam

NOTES 133

in suis ministeriis faciant et iuste omnes sub Dei respectu judicent attendentes." See also notes 47, 52, 55, 56, 69, 151, 235, 239.

CHAPTER III

[192] *Capitularia* (Boretius), I, 69, c. 7: "Si quis corpus defuncti hominis secundum ritum paganorum flamma consumi fecerit et ossa eius ad cinerem redierit, capitae punietur."

[193] *Ibid.*, p. 92, c. 2 concerning the oath of 802: "Precepitque, ut omni [sic] homo in toto regno suo, sive ecclesiasticus sive laicus, unusquisque secundum votum et propositum suum, qui antea fidelitate sibi regis nomine promisissent, nunc ipsum promissum nominis cesaris faciat." Previously, "cunctas generalitas populi" had so promised; *Capitularia* (Boretius), I, 67, c. 4.

[194] *Capitularia* (Krause), II, 278, c. 13: "De fidelitate regi promittenda, id est, omnes per regnum illius Franci fidelitatem illi promittant . . . Ego ille Karolo . . . fidelis ero . . . sicut Francus homo per rectum esse debet suo regi." See Brunner, II, 14.

[195] *Capitularia* (Boretius), I, 272, c. 9: ". . . Et licentiam habeat unusquisque liber homo, qui seniorem non habuerit, cuicumque ex his tribus fratribus [sons of Louis the Pious] voluerit se commendandi."

[196] Waitz, IV, 243–244; Fustel de Coulanges, *Les origines du système féodal*, p. 249; F. Dahn, *Die Könige der Germanen*, VIII, pt. II, 169; Bloch, *La société féodale, les liens de dépendance*, p. 223; F. L. Ganshof, "Benefice and Vassalage," *Cambridge Historical Journal*, VI (1939), 171, n. 114.

[197] Guilhiermoz, pp. 51–52; Dumas, "Le serment de fidélité," *Rev. hist. du droit fr. et étr.*, 4e série, X (1931), 35–36, 42, 295.

[198] Waitz, II, pt. I, 258–259; Brunner, II, 371, n. 10; II, 374 ff.

[199] See preceding note.

[200] Hincmar of Rheims writes to Engilgarius about "hominem tuum Rathramnum . . ., qui tibi servitium debeat"; Flodoard, *Hist. Eccl. Rem.*, lib. III, c. 26 (*SS*, XIII, 546; Migne, *PL*, t. 126, col. 256).

[201] *Actus Pontificum Cenomannis in Urbe Degentium* (Johannes Mabillon, *Vetera Analecta* [new ed., Paris, 1723], p. 289; edited by G. Busson and A. Ledru [Le Mans 1901], p. 263): "Post obitum praefixi Gauzioleni [Abraham] convocavit omnes sodales suos, tam clericos quam et laicos, et dedit illis consilium ut irent ad dominum Carolum, Francorum regem, et sui efficerentur homines, et per eius datum eorum retinerent beneficia. Qui et humana cupiditate seducti, secundum eius consilium fecerunt. Venientes ergo bene parati auro et argento et vestimentis nobilibus ad praedictum regem Francorum, gloriosissimum Carolum, deprecati sunt ut sui mererentur effici homines. Qui et quadam humana cupiditate illusus, suscepit eos, et eorum beneficia sua largitione habere permisit. Monasteria autem

NOTES

et cellulas sive vicos vel villas, quas episcopi ad eorum opus et ad ornandum atque restaurandum sanctam aecclesiam, et ad susceptiones pauperum, seu ad stipendia canonicorum et reliquorum servorum Dei habebant, praedictis hominibus Gauzioleni, quos sibi ad famulandum tunc receperat, sicut antea habebant, habere permisit et aliis suis vasis [sic] in beneficium dedit." *Suscipere* is here plainly used in the technical sense of receive in commendation. These men had already come to Charles and presented their petition to be made his men. He then "received" them, i. e., as his *homines*. The *Actus Pontificum* was written between 840 and 857; see Julien Havet, *Oeuvres* (Paris, 1896), I, 328.

[202] *Vita Sancti Rimberti*, c. 21 (*SS*, II, 774): ". . . circandi episcopatum, placita adeundi, et quando exigeretur, in expeditionem vel ad palatium cum comitatu suo proficiscendi. Nec multo post, electionem succedendi sibi in ipso confirmari, et per manus acceptionem hominem regis illum fieri, et inter consiliarios eius collocari optinuit."

[203] *Annales Fuldenses*, anno 884 (Kurze, p. 113): "Ibi inter alia veniens Zwentibaldus dux cum principibus suis, homo, sicut mos est, per manus imperatoris efficitur, contestatus illi fidelitatem iuramento et, usque dum Karolus vixisset, numquam in regnum suum hostili exercitu esset venturus."

[204] Waitz, II, pt. I, 346.

[205] *Ibid.*, IV, 243-244.

[206] See Waitz's texts.

[207] *Capitularia* (Boretius), I, 325, c. 1: "Ut domnici vassalli qui austaldi sunt et in nostro palatio frequenter serviunt, volumus ut remaneant; eorum homines quos antea habuerunt, qui propter hanc occasionem eis se commendaverunt, cum eorum senioribus remaneant.

[208] *Concessio Generalis*, anno 823 (?), *Capitularia* (Boretius), I, 321, c. 3: "His vero personis quae se nobis commendaverunt, volumus specialiter hoc honoris privilegium concedere prae ceteris liberis, ut in quocumque loco venerint . . . caeteris anteponantur. . . . Et illorum homines liberi qui eis commendati sunt, si ipsi seniores eos secum in servitio habuerint, *etc.*" A similar use of *liber homo* where the phrase has reference to a man who presumably has placed himself in the service of another in a capitulary of Charles the Bald in 873; *Capitularia* (Krause), II, 345: "5. Ut unusquisque comes in suo comitatu provideat, ut, qui fidelitatem nobis adhuc promissam non habent, fidelitatem nobis promittant, sicut in capitulis avi et patris nostri continetur. 6. Ut unusquisque comes in comitatu suo magnam providentiam accipiat, ut nullus liber homo in nostro regno immorari vel proprietatem habere permittatur, cuiuscumque homo sit, nisi fidelitatem nobis promiserit."

[209] For example, *Divisio Regnorum* of 806, *Capitularia* (Boretius), I, 126: "In nomine Patris et Filii et Spiritus sancti. Karolus serenissimus

NOTES 135

augustus, a Deo coronatus magnus pacificus imperator . . . omnibus fidelibus sanctae Dei aecclaesiae ac nostris, praesentibus scilicet et futuris."

[210] A number of citations given by A. Dumas, "Le serment de fidélité," *Rev. hist. de droit fr. et étr.*, 4e série, X (1931), 49, n. 2; 50, n. 1. In the Carolingian period *fideles* replaced the Merovingian *leudes* with which it had been synonymous; Dahn, *Die Könige der Germanen*, VII, pt. I, 189–197; VIII, pt. II, 74; Lot, "Le serment de fidélité à l'époque franque," *Rev. belge de philol. et d'hist.*, XII (1933), 571; Mitteis, *Lehnrecht und Staatsgewalt*, p. 25. Narrow use of *fidelis* for *commendatus* by Lot, *Les destinées de l'empire*, p. 311; p. 651, n. 45; p. 655, n. 72; p. 658; p. 659; p. 668; also by Mitteis, *op. cit.*, p. 61, n. 150.

[211] A diploma of Louis the Pious, anno 836, *HF*, VI, 611: "Imperialis excellentiae magnitudinem decet, fideliter sibi devoteque famulantes muneribus et honoribus ditare." So he concedes certain lands to "Fulberto fideli nostro." See also his diploma for Ecchardus, his *fidelis*, *HF*, VI, 628.

[212] *I Diplomi di Berengario I* (ed. Luigi Schiaparelli, in *Fonti per la storia d'Italia*, XXXV, Rome, 1903), p. 36, anno 890: "Si fidelium nostrorum petitionibus aures clementiae nostrae inclinamus, fideliores ac promtiores eos in nostro esse credimus servitio."

[213] Diploma of Charlemagne, *MGH*, *Diplomata Karolinorum*, I, 291: "propter fidele servitium praedicti fidelis nostri Asig." Diplomas of Charles the Bald for different *fideles*, *HF*, VIII, 435: "sub devotione servitii sui"; *HF*, VIII, 436: "ob devotionem servitii sui." Diploma of Louis the German, *MGH*, *Dipl. Regum Germ. ex Stirpe Karolinorum*, I, 136: "quidam vir fidelisque noster nomine Tuto . . . propter servitium suum."

[214] *Capitula Pistensia* of Charles the Bald, July, 869, *Capitularia* (Krause), II, 333, c. 2: "Ut ab archiepiscopis et episcopis et ab aliis fidelibus nostris honor regius et potestas ac debita obedientia atque adiutorium ad regnum nostrum continendum et defensandum nobis in omnibus et ab omnibus secundum uniuscuiusque ordinem et dignitatem atque possibilitatem, sicut tempore antecessorum nostrorum iuste et rationabiliter consueverat, exhibeatur."

[215] *Capitularia* (Krause), II, 334, c. 3: ". . . Et capitula, quae avus et pater noster pro statu et munimine sanctae Dei ecclesiae ac ministrorum eius et pro pace ac iustitia populi et quiete regni constituerunt, et quae nos cum fratribus nostris regibus et nostris ac eorum fidelibus communiter constituimus . . . permanere inconvulsa decernimus."

[216] As described in Hincmar's *De Ordine Palatii*, c. 29 (ed. M. Prou [Paris, 1884], pp. 72–74; *Capitularia* [Krause], II, 527).

[217] *Capitularia* (Krause), II, 333, c. 3: ". . . omnes nostri fideles . . . qui mihi fideles et obedientes ac veri adiutores atque cooperatores iuxta suum ministerium et personam consilio et auxilio secundum suum scire et

posse et secundum Deum ac secundum seculum fuerint, sicut per rectum unusquisque in suo ordine et statu regi suo et suo seniori esse debet." This capitulary was issued in 869. Similar statements are to be found from 851, *Capitularia* (Krause), II, 73, c. 6; from 860, II, 156, c. 10; from 877, II, 362, c. 2; and repeated by the bishops assembled in council at St. Macrine, in Fismes, April 2, 881, in Mansi, XVII^A, col. 549.

[218] *Capitularia* (Krause), II, 296, anno 858: "Sacramentum fidelium: Quantum sciero et potuero, Domino adiuvante . . . et consilio et auxilio secundum meum ministerium et secundum meam personam fidelis vobis adiutor ero." For a discussion of the content of these oaths see my "Carolingian Oaths of Fidelity," *Speculum*, XVI (1941), 284–296.

[219] *Capitularia* (Krause), II, 278, anno 854: "Ego ille Karolo . . . ab ista die inante fidelis ero secundum meum savirum."

[220] For a discussion of these oaths of fidelity see my article cited above, n. 218. The Merovingians, and subsequently the Carolingians, imposed an oath of fidelity (*fidelitas*) upon all their subjects who thereby promised to be *fideles* (loyal). One might wonder why *fideles* was applied so frequently to a special group within the larger group of subjects, thus leaving out of consideration some men who had sworn to be *fideles* in the oath of fidelity. An answer to such a question must be based on conjecture, but in this case there is a plausible explanation. Men in service are in the *fides* of another; hence they are called *fideles* according to Fustel de Coulanges. Among the Romans, a man who placed himself at the disposal of another, who commended himself to another, established a relationship which was known as *clientela*, *patrocinium*, *tutela*, *amicitia*, but more frequently still, as *fides*; Fustel de Coulanges, *Les origines du système féodal*, pp. 216–220. In the Frankish period *fides* continued to be used although less often, and as we have seen the adjectival form *fideles* is used frequently to designate men who have entered the *fides* or service of another; Fustel de Coulanges, *op. cit.*, p. 249. This background may explain the narrow use of *fideles* in the Merovingian period; this use may certainly have been encouraged by the Carolingian practice in accordance with which the magnates who entered the king's service by commendation supplemented this ceremony with an oath of fidelity. The practice with regard to men who enter the service of "private" lords, men other than the king, appears to be consistent. These men were called upon to swear an oath of fidelity to their lords, although they were not to swear oaths of fidelity to anyone other than their lords and the king; *Capitularia* (Boretius), I, 124, c. 9: "De iuramento, ut nulli alteri per sacramentum fidelitas promittatur nisi nobis et unicuique proprio seniori ad nostram utilitatem et sui senioris." It will be shown below that these men who entered the service of private seigniors could also be called their lord's *fideles*. Thus whether a man commended himself to the king or to another lord, he presumably swore an oath of fidelty and hence might have been called a *fidelis*.

NOTES 137

²²¹ *Ermoldus Nigellus*, lib. IV, 1. 601 ff. (*SS*, II, 512-513):
"Mox manibus iunctis regi se tradidit ultro,
Et secum regnum, quod sibi iure fuit.
Suscipe Caesar, ait, *me, nec non regna subacta:
Sponte tuis memet confero servitiis!*
Caesar at ipse manus manibus suscepit honestis;
Iunguntur Francis Denica regna piis.
Mox quoque Caesar ovans Francisco more veterno
Dat sibi equum nec non, ut solet, arma simul. . . .
Interea Caesar Heroldum iamque fidelem
Munere donat opum pro pietate sua."

²²² *MGH, Diplomata Karolinorum*, I, 242, 1. 5: "Et cum ad nos venisset cum ipsa epistola, quod filius noster ei fecerat, in manibus nostris se commendavit et petivit nobis iam dictus fidelis noster Iohannes, ut ipsum villarem, quod filius noster ei dederat, concedere fecissemus."

²²³ *Ibid.*, I, 241, ll. 40, 44.

²²⁴ We have noted that the expression "to receive" (*suscipere*) someone can mean to receive him into commendation. There is a text which links *suscipere* with *fidelis* in such a way as to lead one to believe that a man who has been "received" has been made a *fidelis*. At the death of Odo, his brother Robert went to Charles the Simple, and after the king had received him honorably, Robert, now made the king's *fidelis*, returned to his own possessions. *Annales Vedastini*, anno 898 (*SS*, I, 531; II, 209): "Posthaec Rodbertus comes, frater regis Odonis, venit ad regem; quem rex honorifice suscepit, eiusque fidelis effectus, rediit ad sua." Ehrenberg, *Commendation und Huldigung*, p. 13, n. 29.

²²⁵ Hincmar of Rheims at the council of Douzy, August, 871; Migne, *PL*, t. 126, col. 598A; Mansi, XVI, 611A: "fideles senioris nostri qui convenimus tam episcopi quam abbates, et comites, et ceteri eius fideles." It will also be shown that men such as these commended themselves.

²²⁶ *Collectio Sangallensis Salomonis III Tempore Conscripta*, No. 34 (*Formulae Merowingici et Karolini Aevi*, edited by Karl Zeumer, Hannover, 1886, p. 418; No. 35 in *Das Formelbuch des Bischofs Salomo III von Konstanz*, edited by Ernst Dümmler, Leipzig, 1857, p. 42): "Ill. N. gratia Dei episcopus N. vicedomino et fideli suo salutem." Dümmler assigns it to the year 877. *Formulae Salzburgenses*, No. 39 (*Formulae*, edited by Zeumer, p. 448): "Ill. gratia Christi donante archiepiscopus ill. ministeriale nostro salutem. Volumus igitur atque precipimus tibi, ut istum indiculum sigillatum, quem ad te dirigamus, ut statim, ut ad te veniet, tu ipse ill. fideli nostro perducas, et de nostra persona dic et verba salutatoria ac fidele servitium, et roga, ut ita perfitiat, sicut in nostro scriptum est indiculo, ita ut in eam confidimus. Et quicquid exinde nobis demandaverit, tu ipse nostris auribus stude promulgare, an ill. nostro vasso sive alio fideli hoc intima, ut ipse nobis indicare valeat missaticum tuum. Vide, ut aliter non

fiet, sed festina hoc perficere sine mora." Actually, a letter of Arno, bishop and later archbishop of Salzburg (785–821); Zeumer, *op. cit.*, p. 438. Earlier examples are given by Waitz, II, pt. I, 347, n. 3.

[227] *Dominus rex* is the ordinary designation of the king; it appears on almost every page of the capitularies. The *dominus* may be regarded as a "courtesy title," in which case it is here translated as "lord"; see F. Lot, "Le serment de fidélité," *Rev. belge de philol. et d'hist.*, XII (1933), 572. Dumas wisely remarks that it is not a meaningless title; only men of considerable eminence, position, and power are addressed as lords (*domini*); see Dumas, "Le serment de fidélité," *Rev. belge de philol. et d'hist.*, XIV^I (1935), 416. *Dominus* is occasionally used with *senior*; Arno of Salzburg refers to the "realm of the lord our seignior"; *MGH, Concilia* (Werminghoff), II, 196: "in regno domni senioris nostri."

[228] Capitulary of 856 addressed to the *fideles* of Charles the Bald in Aquitaine who have revolted, urging those who ought to be his faithful helpers and advisers to be loyal and obedient and helpful just as they ought rightly to be to their king and their seignior; *Capitularia* (Krause), II, 280–281, c. 12: "vos, qui illius [Charles] fideles et consiliarii esse debetis"; c. 7: "fidelis et obediens et adiutor . . . sicut per rectum homo suo regi et suo seniori esse debet." The bishops of the realm of Lothair write in a letter to the bishops of the realm of Charles the Bald in 876, *HF*, VII, 593: "erga nostrum seniorem et regem." See also above, n. 217.

[229] Charter of Robert, count and abbot of St. Martin of Tours, in 895, *HF*, IX, p. 708: "regem dominum et seniorem ac germanum nostrum Odonem." Letter of Hincmar of Laon, Migne, *PL*, t. 124, col. 1028A: "ei . . . domino et seniori ac regi meo."

[230] *Capitularia* (Krause), II, 362, c. 2: "sicut per rectum unusquisque . . . imperatori suo et suo seniori esse debet." In 877.

[231] Capitulary of Meersen, 851; *Capitularia* (Krause), II, 73, c. 6: "sicut per rectum unusquisque . . . suo principi et suo seniori esse debet." Again in 860 at Coblenz, *Capitularia* (Krause), II, 156, c. 10.

[232] Hincmar of Rheims in his *Pro Ecclesiae Libertatum Defensione*, Migne, *PL*, t. 125, col. 1065A, written in 868: "Nos autem fideles vestri, episcopi, et caeteri laicalis ordinis qui adfuerunt . . ." *Capitularia* (Boretius), I, 336, c. 8: "Statuimus de decimis, unde iam inter episcopo seu reliquis sacerdotibus, et comitibus et vassis et reliquis fidelibus nostris multa audivimus intentiones . . ." *Capitularia* (Krause), II, 424: "episcopi et caeteri fideles domni Karoli."

[233] *MGH, Diplomata Regum Germ. ex Stirpe Karolinorum*, II, 192: ". . . Arnaldus fidelis noster, qui nunc est Tullensis ecclesiae episcopus." See also notes 234, 235.

[234] A letter of Louis the Pious, *HF*, VI, 652: "Omnibus episcopis, abbati-

NOTES

bus, abbatissis, comitibus, vicariis, centenariis, seu reliquis fidelibus nostris notum sit . . ."

[235] *MGH, Epistolae*, IV, 528: "Fideles Dei ac nostri, qui hoc egerunt, fuerant ille episcopus, ill. dux, ill. et ill. comites. Ill. dux de Histria, ut dictum est nobis, quod ibidem benefecit ill. cum suis hominibus. Vassi vero nostri fuerunt illi."

[236] See preceding note.

[237] *HF*, VIII, 480: "quemdam fidelem nostrum Vivianum, dilectum et amabilem nobis comitem . . . eidem fideli nostro Viviano . . . praedicto fideli nostro Viviano."

[238] *HF*, VIII, 564: "Porro adnosciri volumus nomina comitatuum, ubi ipsae res sunt, ut fideles nostri, qui comites fuerunt, citius noverint ipsas res sub nostro munimine et defensione consistere." See below, n. 239, 242.

[239] *MGH, Diplomata Karolinorum*, I, 95, l. 13: "nos una cum fidelibus nostris, id est Hagino, Rothlando, Wichingo, Frodegario comitibus nec non et vassis nostris Theodorico, Berthaldo, Albwino, Frodberto, Gunthmaro . . ."

[240] *HF*, VI, 619: "Bavo vassallus noster. . . . Bavo fidelis noster."

[241] *HF*, VIII, 459: "quidam fidelium nostrorum regni Septimaniae vassus noster, nomine Teodtfredus . . . fidelis noster Teodtfredus."

[242] *HF*, VIII, 567: "Proinde nos una cum fidelibus nostris, Vido, Odbertus, Hugo, Davo, Gerardus, Eurebertus, Alcarius, Hubaldus, vassi dominici, seu Gailenus et Fulco comis [sic] palatii et alii plurimi." For another text, see n. 235.

[243] Brunner, II, 233–241.

[244] See above, n. 234.

[245] Remark in the following pages the absence of vassal terms (*vassus, vassallus, vassaticum*) unless the vassals are specifically mentioned in the texts. The relationship between commendation and the oath of fidelity is discussed in Appendix I.

[246] *Annales Bertiniani*, anno 837 (Waitz, p. 15): "Sicque iubente imperatore in sui praesentia episcopi, abbates, comites et vassalli dominici in memoratis locis beneficia habentes Karolo se commendaverunt et fidelitatem sacramento firmaverunt." The bishops are dealt with below, pp. 109 ff.

[247] See below, p. 117 and n. 308, which gives their oath.

[248] These along with one archbishop and seventeen bishops were listed, *Capitularia* (Krause), II, 99–100, as subscribers to the oath given in n. 308.

[249] *Annales Bertiniani*, anno 863 (Waitz, p. 61): "Salomon dux Brittonum cum primoribus suae gentis illi obviam venit seque illi commendat et fidelitatem iurat."

[250] *Ibid.*, anno 877 (Waitz, p. 138); *Capitularia* (Krause), II, 364: "abbates autem et regni primores ac vassalli regii se illi commendaverunt et sacramento secundum morem fidelitatem promiserunt."

NOTES

²⁵¹ *Vita Hludowici Imp.*, c. 59 (*SS*, II, 644): "[Karolo Ludovicus] Neustriam attribuit. . . . Et praesentes quidem Neustriae provintiae primores Karolo et manus dederunt, et fidelitatem sacramento obstrinxerunt, absentium autem quisque postea itidem fecit."

²⁵² *Annales Bertiniani*, anno 838 (Waitz, pp. 15–16).

²⁵³ Text in n. 250 above.

²⁵⁴ Originally *honor* meant office, but by Carolingian times it meant benefices as well; Brunner, II, 107, 344; Bloch, *La société féodale, les liens de dépendance*, pp. 271, 296–298.

²⁵⁵ *Annales Bertiniani*, anno 880 (Waitz, p. 151): "quique de proceribus secundum convenientiam, in cuius divisione honores haberent, illi se commendarent."

²⁵⁶ The Monk of St. Gall, lib. I, c. 11 (*SS*, II, 736) speaks of "comites et praefecti vel diversarum dignitatum proceres." Quoted in n. 88.

²⁵⁷ *Thegani Vita Hludowici*, c. 12 (*SS*, II, 593): "Bernhardus . . . tradidit semetipsum ei *ad procerem*, et fidelitatem cum iuramento promisit." Another manuscript reads *ad obsequium* in place of *ad procerem*.

²⁵⁸ *Einhardi Vita Caroli Magni*, c. 13 (*SS*, II, 450); Fustel de Coulanges, *Transformations*, p. 339, n. 1.

²⁵⁹ Migne, *PL*, t. 122, col. 1302: "omnibus optimatibus regni Caroli gloriosi regis . . . seniorem vestrum."

²⁶⁰ See Brunner, II, 134, and a good chapter in Fustel de Coulanges, *Transformations*, pp. 337–340.

²⁶¹ *Annales Regni Francorum*, anno 806 (Kurze, p. 121): "conventum habuit imperator cum primoribus et optimatibus Francorum de pace constituenda et conservanda inter filios suos et divisione regni facienda in tres partes."

²⁶² See above, n. 257.

²⁶³ *Annales Bertiniani*, anno 845 (Waitz, p. 32): "Karolus . . . Pippinum, Pippini filium suscipit, et receptis ab eo sacramentis fidelitatis, quatenus ita deinceps ei fidelis sicut nepos patruo existeret et in quibuscumque necessitatibus ipsi pro viribus auxilium ferret, totius Aquitaniae dominatum ei permisit, praeter Pictavos, Sanctonas, et Ecolinenses." *Suscipere* is the technical term for "to take into commendation"; see p. 4. Of this Ganshof says, "Pepin se reconnaissait le *vassal* de son oncle"; in Lot, *Les destinées de l'empire*, p. 518; my italics.

²⁶⁴ *Concessio Generalis*, anno 823 (?), *Capitularia* (Boretius), I, 321, c. 3: "His vero personis quae se nobis commendaverunt, volumus specialiter hoc honoris privilegium concedere prae ceteris liberis, ut in quocumque loco venerint, sive ad placitum vel ubicumque, omni honore digni habeantur et caeteris anteponantur; et quicquid ad querendum habuerint, absque ulla dilatione iustitiam suam accipere mereantur." As we have just seen, even royal nephews commended themselves.

NOTES 141

²⁶⁵ *Annales Regni Francorum*, anno 797 (Kurze, p. 100): "Nam ipse ad palatium veniens domno regi semetipsum cum civitate commendavit." He was later exiled; see *Annales Regni Francorum*, anno 801 (Kurze, p. 116).

²⁶⁶ *Annales Regni Francorum*, anno 797 (Kurze, p. 100): "Et in Aquis palatio Abdellam . . . ipso semetipsum commendante suscepit."

²⁶⁷ See Ernst Dümmler, *Geschichte des ostfränkischen Reiches* (2nd ed., Leipzig, 1887), I, 350–352.

²⁶⁸ *Annales Bertiniani*, anno 851 (Waitz, p. 41): "Respogius, filius Nomenogii, ad Karolum veniens, in urbe Andegavorum datis manibus suscipitur."

²⁶⁹ See above, n. 249.

²⁷⁰ *Annales Regni Francorum*, anno 814 (Kurze, p. 141): "Herioldus . . . ad imperatorem venit et se in manus illius commendavit."

²⁷¹ See above, n. 221.

²⁷² *Annales Bertiniani*, anno 862 (Waitz, p. 57): "Welandus ad Karolum veniens, illi se commendavit et sacramenta cum eis quos secum habuit statim praebuit."

²⁷³ *Annales Laureshamenses*, anno 789 (*SS*, I, 34): "tunc Carlus rex iterum per Saxoniam pervenit usque ad Sclavos qui dicuntur Wilti, et venerunt reges terre illius cum rege eorum Tragwito ei obviam, et petita pace tradiderunt universas terras illas sub dominatione Caroli regis Francorum; et dati sunt obsides, et se ipsis traditis, rex reversus est in Francia." The *ipsis traditis* indicates that these kings personally subjected themselves to Charles, probably by an act of commendation since this was the usual form for such princes and since the *ipsis traditis* implies a giving over of their persons. See *loc. cit.* for a probable explanation of the abundance of kings.

²⁷⁴ *Annales Fuldenses, Contin. Ratisbon.*, anno 884 (Kurze, p. 113): "Postea veniente Brazelavoni duce, qui in id tempus regnum inter Dravo et Savo flumine tenuit suique miliciae subditus adiungitur." For *militia* see above, n. 22.

²⁷⁵ See above, n. 203.

²⁷⁶ *Annales Fuldenses*, anno 895 (Kurze, 126): ". . . ibi de Sclavania omnes duces Boemanorum . . . ad regem venientes et honorifice ab eo recepti per manus, prout mos est, regiae potestati reconciliatos se subdiderunt."

²⁷⁷ See pp. 15–17 of the introduction.

²⁷⁸ See n. 246.

²⁷⁹ *Gesta Aldrici Episcopi Cenomannensis, Addimenta* (*SS*, XV, p. 326; Migne, *PL*, t. 115, col. 93A): "[Ludovicus] prefatum [Aldricum] autem pontificem memorato Karolo, filio suo iuniori, per manus commendavit. Cui iam dictus pontifex Aldricus fidem debitam servans . . . a prescripto

episcopio et a sua sede eiectus est." With the revival of the fortunes of Charles, Aldricus later regained his see.

[280] *Annales Bertiniani*, anno 869 (Waitz, p. 101): "sibi [se] [bishops of Verdun, Toul, Metz, Liége] commendantes suscepit; . . . in sua commendatione suscepit." Hincmar of Rheims in addressing these bishops said, *ibid.*, p. 105: "vos ei [Karolo] commendastis."

[281] The reading given certainly follows the text. *Annales Bertiniani*, anno 877 (Waitz, p. 138); *Capitularia* (Krause), II, 364: "Et episcopi se suasque ecclesias illi ad debitam defensionem et canonica privilegia sibi servanda commendaverunt, profitentes secundum suum scire et posse et iuxta suum ministerium consilio et auxilio illi fideles fore; abbates autem et regni primores ac vassalli regii se illi commendaverunt et sacramento secundum morem fidelitatem promiserunt." Brunner (II, p. 68 and his note 29) asserted that there is no example of a bishop commending himself *rechtsförmlich*; his note indicates what he means: that no bishop entered *Kommendation mit Handreichung*, but only "einen Schutz, den der König als solcher den Bischöfen und ihren Kirchen schuldig ist." There is no question as to the fact that Louis II recognized a responsibility to protect his bishops and churches: see *Annales Bertiniani*, anno 877 (Waitz, p. 138), but that in no way exempted them from the responsibility of serving him. As for Brunner's statement (II, 68) that bishops did not commend themselves *mit Handreichung*, it simply is not true; see notes 202, 279, 285, in which the *manus* is specifically mentioned and n. 246 in which there is nothing to indicate that the bishops' commendation or oath of fidelity varied in the slightest particle from that of abbots, counts, and vassals. *Contra* Brunner, Waitz, cited above, n. 23; E. Mayer, *Deutsche und französische Verfassungsgeschichte* (Leipzig, 1899), II, 152, n. 122; Mitteis, *Lehnrecht und Staatsgewalt*, p. 73; Karl Voigt, *Staat und Kirche von Konstatin dem Grossen bis zum Ende der Karolingerzeit* (Stuttgart, 1935), p. 393. Imbart de la Tour (*Les élections épiscopales*, p. 115) says: "Nous ne trouvons pas dans la forme, dans les dispositions essentielles, de différence entre la recommandation des évêques et celle du vassal." See also Ulrich Stutz, "Lehen und Pfrunde," *Zeitschrift der Savignystiftung für Rechtsgeschichte, Germanistische Abteilung*, XX (1899), 234; supposing that men of the Frankish period were capable of fixing the legal source of the bishops' responsibility for service with such finesse, one cannot dispute the fact that bishops generally served the king, and commended themselves like other *fideles* into his service. Episcopal distaste for the swearing of oaths is recognized by Brunner, II, 71, n. 48; concerning the text of 858, see below, Appendix III.

[282] *Capitularia* (Krause), II, 370: "Peticio episcoporum ad domnum Carlomannum regem, quando ei se commendaverunt."

[283] See above, n. 202.

NOTES 143

[284] See above, n. 220, for *fides*.

[285] *Capitularia* (Krause), II, 452, c. 9: "Wenilo in eo consilio et tractatu fuit, ut episcopi, qui mihi fidei promissae debitores erant et consilium atque auxilium manu propria confirmatum ferre debuerant, deficerent et ad fratris mei Hludowici obsequium et subditionem se verterent."

[286] *Capitularia* (Krause), II, 451, c. 1: "In qua parte regni vacabat tunc pastore metropolis Senonum, quam iuxta consuetudinem praedecessorum meorum regum Weniloni tunc clerico meo in capella mea mihi servienti, qui more liberi clerici se mihi commendaverat et fidelitatem sacramento promiserat, consensu sacrorum episcoporum ipsius metropolis ad gubernandum commisi, et apud episcopos, quantum ex me fuit, ut eum ibidem archiepiscopum ordinarent obtinui." This was in 840.

[287] *Capitularia* (Krause), II, 452, c. 13: "Wenilo . . . apud fratrem meum Hludowicum obtinuit, ut vacans episcopatus, Baiocacensis scilicet civitatis, propinquo suo, clerico meo nomine Tortoldo, qui mihi se commendavit et fidelitatem sacramento promisit, donaretur, qui eundum episcopatum in mea infidelitate et contra fidelitatem mihi promissam consensu Hludowici fratris mei accepit."

[288] See above, p. 3 and n. 3.

[289] *Actus Pontificum Cenomannis in Urbe Degentium* (Mabillon, *Vetera Analecta*, p. 290; ed. by Busson and Ledru, p. 264): "Tunc autem domnus Karolus praecepit quendam sacerdotem suum in palacio suo, nomine Hodingum, episcopum ordinari; cui etiam dictum episcopatum ad rigendum [*sic*] commisit. . . . [Hodingus] usque ad domnum Carolum, seniorem suum, pervenire festinandum meruit."

[290] *MGH, Concilia* (Werminghoff), II, 196: "in regno domni senioris nostri."

[291] *MGH, Concilia* (Werminghoff), II, 267: "De clericis . . . in servitio domini nostri."

[292] See above, n. 279.

[293] *Gesta Aldrici*, c. 29 (Migne, *PL*, t. 115, col. 56B): "Accessi humiliter ad clementiam domni senioris nostri Ludovici piissimi imperatoris, petens. . . ."

[294] *Gesta Aldrici*, c. 48 (Migne, *PL*, t. 115, col. 90B; *SS*, XV, 325–326): In the revolt which followed upon the death of Louis the Pious in 840, "Aldricus ecclesiae Cenomanicae episcopus . . . fideliter Karolo seniori suo adhaerebat . . . a praedicto seniore suo se non substraxit; sed inconvulse fidelis et pro viribus adjutor illi exstitit, et propter illum omnia sua dimisit, et eum secutus est per omnia."

[295] St. Rimbert's *Vita Anscharii Hammaburgensis Episcopi* (*HF*, VII, 335): "clementissimi domini et senioris nostri Hludovici regis."

[296] *Capitularia* (Krause), II, 271, c. 1: "nostri seniores."

[297] *Capitularia* (Krause), II, 275–276.

[298] Migne, *PL*, t. 125, col. 813D: "Volumus vos scire, fratres, quia domnus et senior noster, Carolus rex gloriosus . . . petiit . . ." See *Capitularia* (Krause), II, 453.

[299] *HF*, VII, 586: "nostrique senioris domini Hlotharii."

[300] *HF*, VII, 595: "noster senior."

[301] *HF*, VII, 593: "Porro fatemur quia nostro regi fideles sumus, et esse cupimus; cui videlicet fidem de manu patris in regem excepto constanter promisimus . . . Non ergo jura fidei atque Christiani sacramenti erga nostrum seniorem et regem frangere possumus, ne cum mundo aeterna supplica persolvamus."

[302] See above, n. 280.

[303] *HF*, VII, 450; Migne, *PL*, t. 122, col. 1300: "seniorem vestrum." Anno 870.

[304] *HF*, VII, 463–464; Migne, *PL*, t. 126, col. 665–666: ". . . [Carolo] seniore vestro . . . adversus dominum, gentem et populum vestrum."

[305] *Capitularia* (Krause), II, 99; Mansi, XVII[A], col. 310: "cum omnibus episcopis, abbatibus, comitibus ac reliquis, qui nobiscum convenerunt Italici regni optimates."

[306] John VIII had already anointed and crowned him emperor and *augustus* in the Church of St. Peter at Rome, Christmas, 875. See texts in Arthur Kleinclausz, *L'empire carolingien* (Paris, 1902), p. 392, n. 3.

[307] *Capitularia* (Krause), II, 99; Mansi, XVII[A], col. 310: They addressed Charles as "gloriosissimo et a Deo coronato, magno et pacifico imperatori, domno nostro Karolo perpetuo augusto . . . Iam quia divina pietas vos beatorum principum apostolorum Petri et Pauli interventione per vicarium ipsorum, domnum videlicet Iohannem summum pontificem et universalem papam spiritalemque patrem vestrum, ad profectum sanctae Dei ecclesiae nostrorumque omnium incitavit et ad imperiale culmen sancti Spiritus iudicio provexit, nos unanimiter vos protectorem, dominum ac defensorem omnium nostrum et Italici regni regem eligimus."

[308] *Capitularia* (Krause), II, 100: "Sic promitto ego, quia de isto die in antea isti seniori meo, quamdiu vixero, fidelis et obediens et adiutor, quantumcumque plus et melius sciero et potuero, et consilio et auxilio secundum meum ministerium in omnibus ero . . ."

[309] *Capitularia* (Krause), II, 99–100, the list of subscribers.

[310] Mansi, XVIII[A], col. 93, c. xi: ". . . Ideo nobis omnibus complacuit eligere illum [Widonem] in regem et seniorem atque defensorem, quatenus amodo et deinceps illo nos secundum regale ministerium gubernante singuli nostrum in suo ordine obedientes et adiutores pro posse existamus illi ad suam regnique sui salvationem."

[311] *Capitularia* (Krause), II, 348; Mansi, XVII[A], col. 311: "Confirmatio Cisalpinorum . . . Domnum nostrum gloriosum imperatorem Karolum augustum . . . protectorem ac defensorem esse . . . nos qui de Francia,

NOTES 145

Burgundia, Aquitania, Septimania, Neustria, ac Provincia . . . eligimus et confirmamus."

[312] See above, n. 308.

[313] Krause says in *Capitularia*, II, 348: "tum ad exemplum synodi Papiensis, quod attinet ordinem, omnes episcopi—inscriptiones enim iuramento praefixae omnino fictae sunt—Karoli fidem iurarent."

[314] *Capitularia* (Krause), II, 349-350.

[315] The presence of these two legates among those who subscribed to this oath should occasion no surprise. They were in the service of Charles in his newly acquired realm of Italy and so he was also their seignior. John of Arezzo had previously recognized Charles as his seignior at Pavia; his name is among the subscribers there; *Capitularia* (Krause), II, 99. The absence of the name of John of Toscanella is in all probability to be explained by his own absence from that particular meeting.

[316] See above, p. 110 and n. 281.

[317] *Capitularia* (Krause), II, 365: "De ista die et deinceps isti seniori et regi meo Hludowico . . . fidelis et adiutor ero, sicut episcopus recte seniori suo debitor est."

[318] See Heinrich Schrörs, *Hinkmar Erzbischof von Reims* (Freiburg-im-Breisgau, 1884), p. 296.

[319] Migne, *PL*, t. 124, col. 1028A: "ei [Carolo], sicut domino et seniori ac regi meo facere debeo, humiliter satisfaciam."

[320] *Annales Bertiniani*, anno 870 (Waitz, p. 109): "Ego Hincmarus ecclesiae Laudunensis episcopus amodo et deinceps domno seniori meo Karolo regi fidelis et oboediens ero secundum ministerium meum, sicut homo suo seniori et episcopus quilibet [per rectum] suo regi fieri debet."

[321] In his *Pro Ecclesiae Libertatum Defensione* (Migne, *PL*, t. 125, col. 1065A), written in 868: "Nos autem fideles vestri, episcopi, et caeteri laicalis ordinis qui adfuerunt . . . unusquisque profitendo: 'Quantum sciero et potuero . . .'," the *sacramentum fidelium* of 858; *Capitularia* (Krause), II, 296.

[322] At the council of Douzy, August, 871, Migne, *PL*, t. 126, col. 598A; Mansi, XVI, 611A: "fideles senioris nostri qui convenimus tam episcopi quam abbates, et comites, et caeteri eius fideles."

[323] Flodoard describes in detail the letter, *Hist. Eccl. Rem.*, lib. III, c. 26 (*SS*, XIII, 540). Count Gerard had written Hincmar that he had heard that Charles the Bald intended to usurp a monastery which he, Gerard, had founded. Hincmar replies: "adiciens quoque de eo quod se monuerat, ut sacri causa ministerii regem a talibus revocaret excessibus, quia prius in illius suspositione talia non perceperat, et de vanis suspicionibus suum non erat *seniorem* corripere, ideo nec inde monuerat; nunc autem certam et causam habens et personam, debita devotione ac fidelitate studebit dominationem ipsius monere." Schrörs, *Hinkmar*, p. 363, says that

NOTES

Hincmar spoke of the king as *senior* and as justification for this cites three texts, two of which do not offer any proof at all, for they do not apply. In the one case he cites from the *Allocutio duorum episcoporum*, included by Sirmond among the *Opera Hincmari*, I, 753 (Migne, t. 125, col. 813D; see above, n. 298). The unnamed bishops refer to Charles as *senior*, but just who these bishops are we do not know. It is possible that Hincmar of Rheims was one of them, but there is no certain proof of it. In the other case Schrörs cites from Hincmar's *Instructio ad Ludovicum Balbum, Opera Hincmari* (ed. by J. Sirmond [Paris, 1645], II, 183; Migne, *PL*, t. 125, col. 988D). Hincmar in this passage does not refer to anyone as *his own* seignior. In addressing Louis, he speaks of God as "your seignior, king of kings" (*seniore vestro, rege regum*) and he also says that a "homo subjectus . . . vadit . . . cum seniore suo." The third text cited by Schrörs does apply; it is this letter from Hincmar to Gerard, count of Vienne.

[324] Flodoard, *Hist. Eccl. Rem.*, lib. III, c. 23 (*SS*, XIII, 530, l. 23): "non pro Hincmaro, nepote suo, se tantum id dicere asserens, quantum pro ipso seniore suo rege, ne ipse taliter peccaret, unde aeternaliter periret."

[325] Flodoard, *Hist. Eccl. Rem.*, lib. III, c. 22 (*SS*, XIII, 519, ll. 30-31): "Pro quo [Hincmaro Laudunensi Hincmarus Remensis] in tantum laboravit, ut etiam senioris sui regis offensionem incurrisse se dicat."

[326] See n. 226.

[327] As, for example, in notes 201, 202, 203.

[328] It may be asked if *all* men who are in the king's commendation were among his *fideles*. Certainly, as we have seen, all the more important servants were called *fideles*, and perhaps all were. The position of a royal *commendatus*, even of the lowest rank, cannot have been very humble; the king's *commendati* preceded all other free men in honor; see n. 264. Commendation was never used for entrance into an unfree status; see Lot, *Les destinées de l'empire*, p. 667, n. 144, and Fustel de Coulanges, *Les origines du système féodal*, p. 270. It would not be surprising then if *commendati* of the lowest rank were called by the same name as those of the highest rank.

Fustel de Coulanges' rather different usage of *fideles* is discussed in Appendix V.

Chapter IV

[329] J. Calmette, *La société féodale*, p. 36, says that *fideles* are *commendati*, and he asserts that *fideles* and *vassi* are synonymous. It is evident from the above presentation that all *vassi* are *fideles*, but not all *fideles* are *vassi*.

[330] The military character of vassalage was still evident in the eleventh century; Louis Halphen, *L'Essor de l'Europe* (Paris, 1932), p. 7: "Ce qui frappe d'abord, c'est le caractère militaire de ce régime. Vassal, dans les

plus anciens textes de la littérature française, dans nos premières chansons de gestes, est synonyme de guerrier, de vaillant. Le combattant intrépide doit s'élancer 'vassalement' sur l'ennemi; et quand Roland, à Ronceveaux, dans un moment d'abandon, va succomber enfin à la tentation de sonner l'olifant, Olivier l'arrête d'un mot: 'Ne serait vassalage,' c'est-à-dire: Ce ne serait pas d'un brave, ce ne serait pas d'un soldat. Car un 'vassal,' c'est un soldat, le *miles* des Latins; et c'est pourquoi les deux mots *vassalus* et *miles* sont indifféremment employés dans la langue du XIe siècle.

"Mais le 'vassal' n'est pas seulement un soldat; c'est le soldat, le vrai soldat, celui qui seul compte dans la bataille aux yeux des hommes de ce temps; l'homme qui combat à cheval, armé de l'épée, de la lance et de l'écu."

[331] *Contra* the following historians: Declareuil, see above, n. 13; Pfister and Pirenne, see above, p. 7; Poupardin, Ganshof, Esmein, Viollet, Calmette, Petot, Pöschl, see above, n. 17; Waitz, see above, p. 10; Guilhiermoz, see above, p. 12; Fustel de Coulanges, see above, p. 15; Imbart de la Tour, see above, p. 17; Dahn, see below, p. 139; Dumas, see below, p. 141; Lot, see below, p. 142; Bloch, see below, p. 143; Brunner, see below, p. 145; Stephenson, see below, n. 391; Lesne, see below, p. 146. Mitteis, see above, p. 13, comes closest to the point of view presented in this study.

[332] See above, n. 54.

[333] See n. 73.

[334] Guilhiermoz, pp. 49–77.

[335] In agreement with J. Calmette, *La société féodale*, pp. 16–17; Alfons Dopsch, 'Beneficialwesen und Feudalität,' *Mitteilungen der österreichischen Instituts für Geschichtsforschung*, XLVI, 16–20; E. Mayer, *Deutsche und französische Verfassungsgeschichte*, II, 148–149; F. Dahn, *Die Könige der Germanen*, VIII, pt. II, 180.

[336] Lot, *Les destinées de l'empire*, pp. 643–646.

[337] *Ibid.*, pp. 648–652.

[338] *Ibid.*, pp. 657–661.

[339] The case of Tassilo, see above, n. 119.

[340] See notes 203, 246, 249, 250, 251, 257, 272, 281, 286, 287. Louis the Pious has gone into Aquitaine to establish his son Charles as king in that region; the emperor and Charles meet the Aquitanians; *Annales Bertiniani*, anno 839 (Waitz, p. 23): "Quos filio suo Karolo more patrio commendatos, sibi eidemque filio suo sacramento interpositione firmavit." Referring to the same event, *Nithardi Hist.*, I, c. 8 (*SS*, II, 655): "Et quoniam olim regnum Aquitaniae Carolo donaverat, ut illi se commendarent, ortando suasit, iussit. Qui omnes commendati, eidem sacramento fidem firmaverunt." *Annales Bertiniani*, anno 858 (Waitz, p. 49): "Berno dux partis pyratarum Sequanae insistentium ad Karlum regem in Vermeria palatio venit, eiusque se manibus dedens, fidelitatem statim iurat."

[341] See n. 246.

[342] For a full discussion of the content of these oaths, see my article "Carolingian Oaths of Fidelity," *Speculum*, XVI (1941), 284–296.

An example of the subject's oath, that of 854, *Capitularia* (Krause), II, 278, c. 13: "Sacramentum autem fidelitatis tale est: Ego ille Karolo, Hludowici et Iudit filio, ab ista die inante fidelis ero secundum meum savirum, sicut Francus homo per rectum esse debet suo regi. Sic me Deus adiuvet et istae reliquiae."

An example of the oath sworn by the magnates, that at Kiersy in 858, *Capitularia* (Krause), II, 296: "Quantum sciero et potuero, Domino adiuvante absque ulla dolositate aut seductione et consilio et auxilio secundum meum ministerium et secundum meam personam fidelis vobis adiutor ero, ut illam potestatem, quam in regio nomine et regno vobis Deus concessit, ad ipsius voluntatem et ad vestram ac fidelium vestrorum salvationem cum debito et honore et vigore tenere et gubernare possitis; et pro ullo homine non me inde retraham, quantum Deus mihi intellectum et possibilitatem donaverit."

[343] J. Flach, *Les origines de l'ancienne France*, II, 523.

[344] A. Esmein, *Cours élémentaire* . . . (15th ed. by R. Génestal, Paris, 1930), p. 190, n. 11.

[345] Lot has been interpreted in this sense by Dumas, "Encore la question: 'Fidèles ou vassaux?'," *Nouv. rev. hist. de droit fr. et étr.*, XLIV (1920), 215, 216. Lot insisted upon the necessary union of the two ceremonies; *Fidèles ou vassaux?* (Paris, 1904), p. 247: "C'est par leur [l'hommage et la fidélité] union intime, indissoluble, que précisément se forme l'engagement vassalique." Again, *op. cit.*, p. 248: "Le contrat vassalique résultant précisément de l'union de la fidélité avec l'hommage, il est clair que vouloir séparer l'un de l'autre dans l'étude du régime féodal c'est tomber dans un pur nonsens." In the very next paragraph, however, Lot says that it is the oath of fidelity which indicates the bearing and meaning of the act of homage; *op. cit.*, p. 249: "L'hommage à lui seul ne constituant pas la vassalité, doit être suivi d'un acte précisant le sens et la portée de la 'tradition' que le *vassus* vient de faire de sa personne, et c'est à quoi répond le serment de fidélité." Lot's later references to this subject in Lot, Pfister, and Ganshof, *Les destinées de l'empire*, are not very helpful; he says on one occasion (p. 651) that the ceremony of homage was accompanied by an oath of fidelity, and a little later (p. 666) he remarks that the oath of fidelity was accompanied by an act of homage.

[346] Auguste Dumas, *Nouv. rev. hist. de droit fr. et étr.*, XLIV (1920), 198.

[347] *Ibid.*, 215–217; same position briefly in Dumas, "Le serment de fidélité, etc.," *Rev. hist. de droit fr. et étr.*, 4e série, X (1931), 301. Strangely enough, although Dumas places such strong emphasis on the oath of fidelity, the act which gives meaning and content to the empty form of commenda-

tion, he insists that there is no difference between the oath of fidelity of the subject and that of the magnate who is a *commendatus*. The latter is bound to his seignior no more tightly than the subject is bound to his king. Still, there is a difference in the measure of obligation which these men feel. Dumas seeks to explain this by saying that the magnate feels bound toward the king *non pas plus étroitement, mais plus sérieusement,* for he commends himself to the king and promises his fidelity in person to the flesh and blood king; the subject, on the other hand, promises his fidelity indirectly to an intermediary sent by the king; *ibid.,* 46–50. This explanation would seem to make the "essential" ingredients or distinguishing features of the "vassalage" relationship commendation and personal contact rather than the oath of fidelity, which, according to Dumas, is the same whether sworn by a simple subject or by a man rendering homage. For a full discussion of this aspect of Dumas' theory, see my "Carolingian Oaths of Fidelity," *Speculum,* XVI (1941), 284–296.

[348] Guilhiermoz, pp. 77–85, 255–256, 341, 446.

[349] Petot, "L'hommage servile," *Rev. hist. de droit fr. et étr.,* 4e série, VI (1927), 90, 91.

[350] *Ibid.,* 96.

[351] *Ibid.,* 98.

[352] Marc Bloch, *La société féodale, la formation des liens de dépendance* (Paris, 1939), 226.

[353] Waitz, IV, 248.

[354] *Ibid.*

[355] Ehrenberg, *Commendation und Huldigung,* pp. 131–133, 140; Guilhiermoz, p. 78, n. 3.

[356] As in notes 246 and 340.

[357] *Contra,* Bloch, *op. cit.,* p. 226: "Nous ne connaissons pas d'hommages sans foi."

[358] See above, n. 222.

[359] *Concessio Generalis,* anno 823 (?), *Capitularia* (Boretius), I, 321, c. 3: "His vero personis quae se nobis commendaverunt, volumus specialiter hoc honoris privilegium concedere prae ceteris liberis, ut in quocumque loco venerint . . . caeteris anteponantur. . . . Et illorum homines liberi qui eis commendati sunt, si ipsi seniores eos secum in servitio habuerint, *etc.*"

[360] See note 279.

[361] See note 280.

[362] See note 202.

[363] See note 255.

[364] Dahn, *Die Könige der Germanen,* VIII, pt. II, 171, says that the oath customarily (one cannot assert more) followed commendation.

[365] Esmein, *op. cit.,* p. 190; J. Calmette, *La société féodale* (4th ed., Paris, 1938), pp. 38, 39.

NOTES

³⁶⁶ Dahn, *op. cit.*, VII, pt. III, 399: "Der Eid kann immer nur religiös bekräftigen, was als rechtliche oder sittliche Verpflichtung bereits besteht oder jetzt anerkannt wird."

³⁶⁷ Calmette, *op. cit.*, p. 38: "Les éléments du problème énoncé sont les suivants: dans le cérémonial, la foi vient après l'hommage; l'hommage se prête *per manus*, la foi, par serment; aucun texte ne permet de faire un départ quelconque entre des obligations qui naîtraient de la foi et des obligations qui naîtraient de l'hommage; à prendre les documents à la lettre, tantôt il semblerait que les devoirs dérivent de la foi, tantôt que les mêmes devoirs dérivent de l'hommage. Dès lors, il apparaît que la question qui consiste à se demander si c'est la foi ou si c'est l'hommage qui engendre les obligations féodales n'a pas de sens historiquement. L'hommage et la foi sont deux moments d'un acte unique, l'acte créateur du lien féodal. C'est de l'acte en son entier, non du premier moment de l'acte (hommage) ou du second (foi), que naissent les devoirs féodaux."

³⁶⁸ Fustel de Coulanges, *Les origines du système féodal*, p. 288.

³⁶⁹ *Capitularia* (Boretius), I, 124, c. 9: "De iuramento, ut nulli alteri per sacramentum fidelitas promittatur nisi nobis et unicuique proprio seniori ad nostram utilitatem et sui senioris."

³⁷⁰ In agreement with Brunner, II, 365; *contra*, Petot, *Rév. hist. de droit fr. et étr.*, 4e série, VI (1927), 96, n. 1.

³⁷¹ See above, n. 220 and n. 226.

³⁷² See above, notes 119, 203, 246, 249, 250, 251, 257, 272, 281, 286, 287, 340. The bishops in the mid-ninth century and after preferred to give a *promise* of fidelity rather than an *oath* of fidelity, but the content of the promise was the same as that of the oath of the other *fideles*; see Appendix III.

³⁷³ F. Dahn, *Die Könige der Germanen*, VIII, pt. II, 158.

³⁷⁴ *Ibid.*, VIII, pt. II, 171.

³⁷⁵ *Ibid.*, VIII, pt. II, 172: "Erst sehr allmählig wird in karolingischer Zeit der Treueid Wesensform, und zwar nicht für jede Commendation, nur für die in das Vassaticum." What was the essential form before the addition of the oath?

³⁷⁶ *Ibid.*, VIII, pt. II, 173.

³⁷⁷ *Ibid.*, VIII, pt. II, 182–183: "Wie bei dem Ausdruck *ministerialis* macht es auch sonst oft grosse Schwierigkeiten, zumal seit a. 814 und a. 840, das Verhältnis von Vassallität und Amt zu unterscheiden: in vielen Fällen ist nicht ersichtlich, ob die Quellen das Eine oder das Andere oder beides— in Personal-Union—meinen: letzeres ist häufig, da eben jetzt fast alle (zumal höhere) Beamte Vassallen geworden waren, andrerseits der König heimgefallene Aemter am liebsten Vassallen gab und beiden—auch abgesehen von den herkommlichen Amtsbeneficien—heimgefallene Beneficien. Dazu kam, das die Vassallen, auch wenn sie nicht Beamte sind, ganz ähnliche

NOTES

Pflichten, Rechte, Vorzüge haben. Es wird vorausgesetzt, dass Bischöfe, sogar Priester, nicht nur Aebte und Grafen, Vassallen sind; daneben werden selbstverständlich auch wieder Bischöfe, Aebte, Grafen und Kronvassallen neben einander gestellt, grade um Allen, auch falls sie nicht Vassallen sind, gleiche Pflichten, z. B. Eide, aufzulegen. Ferner beginnt das Wort *honor*, früher nur für Amt gebraucht, allmälig auch *beneficium* zu bedeuten, so dass nunmehr auch alle die Stellen, in denen *honores* übertragen oder verwirkt werden, mehr Schwierigkeit als Klarheit darüber gewähren, ob Amt oder *beneficium* oder beides, zumal ob das Amt selbst als *beneficium* gemeint sei. Dass damals schon jeder Beamte Vassall werden musste, ist nicht anzunehmen, wohl aber war das längst Regel, wenn er dabei ein Amtsbeneficium (oder ein anderes) empfing."

378 *Ibid.*, VIII, pt. II, 184: "die Undurchsichtigkeit der Verhältnisse."

379 Auguste Dumas, "Encore la question: 'Fidèles ou vassaux?'," *Nouv. rev. hist. de droit fr. et étr.*, XLIV (1920), 197: "L'engagement vassalique est l'acte par lequel un homme libre se met au service d'un autre homme libre."

380 *Ibid.*, 203: "Assurément c'est le roi qui, au début, réunit le groupe de vassaux le plus considérable et qui a tracé la voie aux *potentes*. Les textes appellent ces vassaux du roi, *vassi dominici* ou *vassi regales*. Nourris dans le palais ou chasés sur des bénéfices qui leur ont été concédés, ils sont à la disposition du prince pour remplir toutes les missions qu'il juge à propos de leur confier: on peut les considérer comme de véritables fonctionnaires royaux. Ce sont parfois des personnages de haut rang qui ont leur place immédiatement après les comtes." Similar statement in Dumas, "Le serment de fidélité à l'époque franque, réponse à M. Lot," *Rev. belge de philol. et d'hist.*, XIV (1935), 418-419.

381 Dumas, *Nouv. rev. hist. de droit fr. et étr.*, XLIV (1920), 203-204: "D'ailleurs, au IXe siècle, tous les grands sont assimilés à des vassaux royaux. Sans doute, il est rare que les textes donnent explicitement cette qualité aux ducs, comtes, évêques et abbés: ces hauts dignitaires ont une position plus élevés que les simples *vassi dominici*; aussi sont-ils généralement énumérés à part. Mais la solennité dans laquelle s'affirme la fidélité envers le roi est la même pour tous: c'est l'hommage suivi d'un serment. Peut-être les Carolingiens comptent-ils que cette cérémonie humiliante est susceptible d'accroître le dévouement de chacun."

382 Lot, *Les destinées de l'empire*, p. 673: "La fonction publique devient vassalique. La vassalité supplante les autres formes de la *commendatio*. Les grands personnages de l'état, ducs, comtes, marquis, évêques, abbés, prêtent l'hommage au souverain, comme de simples vassaux."

383 *Ibid.*, p. 668: "[Les Carolingiens] ont voulu que ses dévoués, les *vassi dominici*, fussent honorés et respectés des populations à l'égal des comtes, évêques, abbés."

NOTES

[384] *Ibid.*, p. 673, n. 175: "Les fils ou neveux du roi sont considérés comme ses vassaux."

[385] Bloch, *La société féodale, les liens de dépendance*, pp. 233-245.

[386] *Ibid.*, p. 227: "Car, malgré de grandes diversités de richesse et de prestige, les vassaux ne se recrutaient point indifféremment parmi toutes les couches de la population. La vassalité était la forme de dépendance propre aux classes supérieures, que distinguaient, avant tout, la vocation guerrière et celle du commandement."

[387] *Ibid.*, pp. 245-246: "Il y eut plus: ce lien de vassalité, dont l'expérience semblait prouver la force, les Carolingiens s'avisèrent de l'employer à s'assurer la fidélité éternellement chancelante de leurs fonctionnaires. Ceux-ci avaient toujours été conçus comme placés sous le 'maimbour' spécial du souverain; ils lui avaient toujours prêté serment; ils étaient, de plus en plus fréquemment, recrutés parmi des hommes qui, avant de recevoir de lui cette mission, l'avaient servi comme vassaux. La pratique peu à peu se généralisa. Au moins à partir du règne de Louis le Pieux, il n'est plus de charge de cour ni de grand commandement, plus de comté notamment, dont le titulaire n'ait dû, au plus tard à son entrée en dignité, se faire, jointes mains, le vassal du monarque. Des princes étrangers eux-memes, s'ils reconnaissent le protectorat franc, on exige, dès le milieu du VIIIe siècle, qu'ils se soumettent à cette cérémonie et on les dit, à leur tour, les vassaux du roi ou de l'empereur. Certes, de tous ces hauts personnages nul n'attendait que, comme les suivants d'autrefois, ils montassent la garde dans la demeure du maître. À leur façon pourtant, ils appartenaient à sa maison militaire, puisqu'ils lui devaient, avant tout, avec leur foi, l'aide de guerre.

"Or les grands, de leur côté, s'étaient depuis longtemps habitués à voir dans les bons compagnons qui formaient leurs bandes des hommes de confiance, prêts aux missions les plus diverses. . . . Seigneurs comme subordonnés ne pouvaient manquer d'aller naturellement vers une forme de contrat qui, désormais, était pourvue de sanctions légales. Par les liens de la vassalité les comtes s'attachèrent les fonctionnaires d'ordre inférieur; l'évêque ou l'abbé, les laïques qu'ils chargeaient de les aider à rendre la justice ou de conduire à l'armée leurs sujets."

[388] *Ibid.*, p. 296: "Dès les premiers Carolingiens, on l'a vu, le roi s'attachait par les liens de la vassalité les personnages auxquels il confiait les principales charges de l'État et, notamment, les grands commandements territoriaux, comtés, marches ou duchés."

[389] Heinrich Brunner, *Deutsche Rechtsgeschichte*, II (2nd ed., Munich and Leipzig, 1928), 349-368, *passim*.

[390] *Ibid.*, II, 109: "Die Karolinger bewerstelligten eine Reform des unter den Merowingern völlig verwilderten Beamtentums. Als eines der Mittel strengerer Unterordnung diente ihnen die Massregel, dass sie die höheren Amter zum Teil mit ihren Vasallen besetzten und den Eintritt von höheren

NOTES

Beamten in die Vasallität beförderten oder veranlassten." Also *ibid.*, II, 368: "Die Ergebung der Beamten in die Vasallität und die Besetzung der höheren Ämter mit königlichen Vasallen hatte die Umwandlung des Amtsgutes und schliesslich des Amtes in ein Benefizium zur Folge." See also *ibid.*, II, 344.

[391] Carl Stephenson. "The Origin and Significance of Feudalism," *American Historical Review*, XLVI (1941), 806–808. After describing the military character of vassalage, he says that "by the end of the ninth century the more important agents of the state had been brought within the category of royal vassals." Stephenson presents no documentation for this assertion; he continues, "The transition was an informal one, of which the capitularies tell us little, but that the result was quite in accord with Carolingian policy seems clear."

[392] Brunner, II, 71.

[393] A. Dopsch, *Grundlagen der europäischen Kulturentwicklung* (2nd ed., Vienna, 1923–1924), II, 304: "Die Begründung des Vasallitätsverhältnisses erfolgte noch in fränkischer Zeit durch Kommendation."

[394] A. Dopsch, *Wirtschaftsentwicklung der Karolingerzeit* (2nd ed., Weimar, 1921–1922), I, 231.

[395] A. Dopsch, *Wirtschaftsentwicklung*, I, 229: "Die meisten der königlichen Benefiziare waren zugleich auch Vasallen des Königs oder, falls es sich um Geistliche oder Frauen handelte, ihm doch zu Treue und Dienst auch sonst verpflichtet." He has made this distinction to avoid the conclusion that clerics and women were vassals. That the difficulty arises from his identification of commendation with vassalage is clear from *Grundlagen*, II, 332. See above, n. 72.

[396] Emile Lesne, *Histoire de la propriété ecclésiastique en France*, II[2] (Lille, 1926), 86: "Les évêques en effet sont des *fidèles*; le roi les range comme tels à côté des abbés, des comtes et de ses autres fidèles. Comme tous les autres, les évêques lui prêtent serment et se placent dans la recommendation." This statement is quite correct in my opinion for reasons already made evident.

[397] *Ibid.*, II[1] (Lille, 1922), 131: "Quand les Capitulaires et les Annales énumèrent les diverses catégories des fidèles royaux, on y voit figurer les prélats à côté des comtes et des autres *vassi*. La personne de l'évêque, de l'abbé pouvait-elle être épargnée par la marée montante des idées et institutions vassaliques qui envahissent toute la société de ce temps?. . . . Les liens nouveaux qui rattachent les églises à la couronne et les prélats à la personne royale, les assujettissent aussi à des charges et à des devoirs inconnus à l'âge antérieur."

[398] *Ibid.*, II[2], 413: "Offrir des dons au souverain est un devoir qui s'impose semblablement aux comtes et à tous les hommes du roi. Les chefs des églises y sont tenus au même titre que les autres fidèles. Évêques et abbés

acquittent les *annua dona* des vassaux. Si les recteurs des églises ont été astreints à cette régulière contribution, dont il n'est pas trace avant l'époque carolingienne, c'est pour une part la conséquence du développement de la vassalité, qui crée aux prélats des obligations nouvelles vis à vis du roi, leur *senior*."

[399] *Ibid.*, II², 88: "On ne considère pas les évêques comme des *vassi* du roi, bien qu'ils lui aient prêté serment." But this was apparently only a case of "musn't say the nasty word": "Sur ces points, les *formes du langage* respectent les habitudes et les règles de la discipline ecclésiastique, en dépit de l'envahissement par le droit royal de l'ancienne législation canonique."

[400] Victor Ehrenberg, *Commendation und Huldigung* (Weimar, 1877), pp. 12–13.

[401] *Ibid.*, p. 14: "Es giebt nämlich auch unfreie Vassallen, d. h. Knechte, die kraft einseitigen Willensactes ihres Eigenthümers Vassallen geworden sind." Hence *Commendation* rather than *Vassalität* in the title of his book.

[402] *Ibid.*, pp. 15, 16.

[403] *Ibid.*, p. 78.

[404] For the narrative see Dümmler, *Geschichte des ostfränkischen Reiches*, I, 426–443; Joseph Calmette, *La diplomatie carolingienne* (*Bibliothèque de l'École des hautes études*, fasc. 135, Paris, 1901), pp. 36–59.

[405] *Capitularia* (Krause), II, 427–441.

[406] *Capitularia* (Krause), II, 428.

[407] *Capitularia* (Krause), II, 439.

[408] *Capitularia* (Krause), II, 428, c. 1; 438, c. 15.

[409] Hincmar of Rheims said as much in a letter to Charles the Bald; see *Capitularia* (Krause), II, 428.

[410] *Capitularia* (Krause), II, 439: "'Talem nempe vos debemus et volumus credere, ut nec vos regni augmentum cum animae vestrae detrimento velitis habere necque nos cum tali dedecore ad adiutorium ecclesiastici regiminis et gubernationis recipere, ut sine sacerdotio simus, quo privati erimus, si contra Deum et rationis auctoritatem nos ecclesiasque nostras vobis studuerimus committere. Ecclesiae siquidem nobis a Deo commissae non talia sunt beneficia et huiusmodi regis proprietas, ut pro libitu suo inconsulte illas possit dare vel tollere, quoniam omnia, quae ecclesiae sunt, Deo consecrata sunt. Unde qui ecclesiae aliquid fraudatur aut tollit, sacrilegium secundum sanctam scripturam facere noscitur. Et nos episcopi Domino consecrati non sumus huiusmodi homines, ut, sicut homines saeculares, in vassallatico debeamus nos cuilibet commendare—sed ad defensionem et ad adiutorium gubernationis in ecclesiastico regimine nos ecclesiasque nostras committere—aut iurationis sacramentum, quod nos evangelica et apostolica atque canonica auctoritas vetat, debeamus quomodo facere. Manus enim chrismate sacro peruncta, quae de pane et vino aqua mixto per orationem et crucis signum conficit corpus et Christi san-

NOTES 155

guinis sacramentum, abhominabile est, quicquid ante ordinationem fecerit, ut post ordinationem episcopatus saeculare tangat ullomodo sacramentum. Et lingua episcopi, quae facta est per Dei gratiam clavis caeli, nefarium est, ut, sicut saecularis quilibet, super sacra iuret in nomine Domini et sanctorum invocatione. . . ."

[411] Earlier in the same letter they referred to "real" vassals; *Capitularia* (Krause), II, 432, c. 7: "Quapropter, sicut et illae res ac facultates, de quibus vivunt clerici, ita et illae sub consecratione immunitatis sunt, de quibus debent militare vasalli. . . ." These are the vassals whose revenues are derived from lands of the church. Hincmar of Rheims, actual author of the letter sent by the bishops, thought of *vassaticum* in connection with fighting; see n. 73 above.

[412] Imbart de la Tour, *Les élections épiscopales*, p. 113, translates "sed ad defensionem et ad adiutorium gubernationis in ecclesiastico regimine nos ecclesiasque nostras committere" as "pour obtenir de lui [king] pour eux et leur église sa défense et son secours"; this is similar to that of Lesne, *Histoire de la propriété ecclésiastique*, II², 87, "confier leur personne et leurs églises au roi pour qu'il les défende et les assiste dans le gouvernement ecclésiastique." In both translations the one who does the helping is the king. Notice, however, that the text says that they commend themselves "for defense and help in governing ecclesiastical affairs." This could mean either that the king helped the bishops or that the bishops helped the king in governing ecclesiastical affairs. We are not to assume at this date that the state and the church are two separate hostile administrations; king and bishops work together for the church and state. Just before this sentence the bishops had said that if they were deprived of their proper sacerdotal character, Louis would not wish "nos cum tali dedecore ad adiutorium ecclesiastici regiminis et gubernationis recipere," to receive men in such disgrace for help in ecclesiastical administration and government. According to this, the king receives the men who help him in ecclesiastical affairs. If the phrase which can be translated in either way is to coincide with this one and the statement that they do not commend themselves in vassalage, then it must be translated that the bishops commend themselves to the king to help in ecclesiastical affairs. That is just what they wish to impress upon him at this moment to avoid taking a stand in more secular politics.

[413] Brunner, II, 71, n. 48.

[414] *Capitularia* (Krause), II, 342: "Professio episcoporum. Quantum sciero et potuero adiuvante Domino consilio et auxilio secundum meum ministerium fidelis vobis adiutor ero, ut regnum, quod vobis Deus donavit vel donaverit, ad ipsius voluntatem et sanctae ecclesiae ac debitum regium honorem vestrum et vestram fideliumque vestrorum salvationem habere et obtinere et continere possitis.

"Sacramentum laicorum. Quantum sciero et potuero adiuvante Domino consilio et auxilio fidelis vobis adiutor ero, ut regnum, quod habetis ad Dei voluntatem et sanctae ecclesiae et vestrum honorem atque ad vestram salvationem continere possitis, et quod Deus adhuc vobis concesserit, adquirere et contra omnes homines defendere valeatis."

[415] See the text from the *Annales Bertiniani*, anno 877, quoted above in n. 281.

[416] Waitz, IV, 283.

[417] Waitz, IV, 248.

[418] Brunner, II, 71; see also above, n. 281. F. Dahn, *Die Könige der Germanen*, VIII, pt. II, 183.

[419] Imbart de la Tour, *Les élections épiscopales*, p. 113.

[420] Lesne, *Histoire de la propriété ecclésiastique*, II², 87.

[421] Mitteis agrees with this point of view; *Lehnrecht und Staatsgewalt*, p. 74: "Ein ernstlicher Widerstand [by the bishops] gegen die Kommendation [for Mitteis, vassalage] findet sich nicht. Meist wird dafür das bekannte Schreiben der westfränkischen Bischöfe von der Synode zu Quierzy (858) angeführt, aus dem man allerdings schliessen müsste, das ihnen und ihrem geistigen Führer Hinkmar v. Reims der Kommendationsritus als ein ganz besonders schwerer Verstoss gegen die priesterliche Würde erschienen sei. Aber man darf nie vergessen, das dieser Brief an einen Usurpator gerichtet war, der mit seinen Truppen in Feindesland stand, und der Stellung der Bischöfe gegenüber dem westfränkischen König nicht präjudizierte; nicht gegen die Huldigung an sich, nur gegen die erzwungene Huldigung mit ihren schweren äusseren und inneren Konflikten suchen die Bischöfe Schutz unter dem Mantel kanonischer Rechtsanschauungen."

[422] They did seek to set limits upon the necessity of obedience *in omnibus* by encouraging a political theory which limited the power of the king; see my article.

[423] *Untersuchungen zum fränkischen Benefizialrecht* (Weimar, 1937), pp. 48–65.

[424] *Ibid.*, pp. 55, 56.

[425] *Annales Regni Francorum* (Kurze, pp. 14–17), anno 757.

[426] Krawinkel, *op. cit.*, p. 50.

[427] *Ibid.*, p. 50.

[428] *Ibid.*, p. 51.

[429] *Ibid.*, p. 54.

[430] *Ibid.*, p. 51.

[431] *Ibid.*, p. 52.

[432] *Annales Regni Francorum* (Kurze), pp. 20–23.

[433] Krawinkel, *op. cit.*, p. 52.

[434] *Ibid.*, p. 57.

[435] *Ibid.*, p. 55.

[436] See above, n. 78.

NOTES

⁴³⁷ Krawinkel, *op. cit.*, p. 55, n. 2.

⁴³⁸ *Annales Regni Francorum* (Kurze, p. 78), anno 787; see above, n. 138.

⁴³⁹ *Annales Regni Francorum* (Kurze, p. 79), anno 787: "Nam videns se undique circumsessum, venit supplex ac veniam de ante gestis sibi dari deprecatus est. Sed et rex, sicut erat natura mitissimus, supplici ac deprecanti pepercit acceptisque ab eo praeter filium eius Theodonem aliis, quos ipse imperavit, duodecim obsidibus et populo terrae per sacramenta firmato in Franciam reversus est."

⁴⁴⁰ *Annales Regni Francorum* (Kurze, pp. 80–81), anno 788.

⁴⁴¹ Krawinkel, *op cit.*, p. 57.

⁴⁴² Fustel de Coulanges, *Transformations*, p. 353.

⁴⁴³ Fustel de Coulanges, *Les origines du système féodal*, pp. 248–249.

⁴⁴⁴ *Capitularia*, I (Boretius), 44: "Apostolicae sedis hortatu, omniumque fidelium nostrorum, et maxime episcoporum ac reliquorum sacerdotum." In 807 he issues a capitulary with regard to fasting after consulting with his *fideles*, lay and spiritual, and after obtaining from both their advice and consent; *Capitularia*, I (Boretius), 245: "nos, cum fidelibus nostris tam spiritalibus quam saecularibus tractantes, cum consensu et pari consilio invenimus."

⁴⁴⁵ Examples of the *optimates, proceres, primores* among the *fideles* are given above, pp. 103–106.

⁴⁴⁶ See citation in n. 443. Ganshof, "Benefice and Vassalage," *Cambridge Historical Review*, VI (1939), 151, n. 23, n. 24, thinks that the term *fideles* underwent an evolution in the period under consideration here; in the latter part of the ninth century and even more in the tenth century it came to mean "vassal." In the time of Charlemagne, however, he says that it had only the general meaning of "subject"; he admits, though, that often the *fideles* of the texts were vassals, "but this we only know through some special mention in the texts, as, for example, from the fact that they are specified as *fideles* holding benefices from the king." It must be admitted, of course, that *fidelis* can mean "subject." It still remains for Ganshof to prove that it can mean only "subject." Such a notion is contrary to the general opinion that there are two uses for the term; see authors cited in n. 210. Whenever there are two usages for a term, the context has to indicate which usage is meant. Ganshof himself cites a case of *fideles nostri discurrentes* in Italy in 776, "who appear to be men charged with some particular mission" and thus not ordinary subjects. The text of 769 or a little later, cited above in n. 444, shows Charlemagne being advised by all his *fideles*; these surely are not his subjects. Context reveals later a narrow use of *fidelis*; it likewise reveals a narrow use in the time of Charlemagne.

FREQUENT ABBREVIATIONS

Brunner	Heinrich Brunner, *Deutsche Rechtsgeschichte*, I (2nd edition, Leipzig, 1906); II (2nd edition revised by Claudius Freiherr von Schwerin, Munich and Leipzig, 1928).
Capitularia (Boretius) I	Alfred Boretius, ed., *Capitularia Regum Francorum*, vol. I (Hannover, 1883) of *Legum Sectio II* of *Monumenta Germaniae Historica*.
Capitularia (Krause), II	Alfred Boretius and Victor Krause, ed., *Capitularia Regum Francorum*, vol. II (Hannover, 1897) of *Legum Sectio II* of *Monumenta Germaniae Historica*.
Concilia (Werminghoff)	Albert Werminghoff, ed., *Concilia Aevi Karolini* (Hannover and Leipzig, 1906–1908), vol. II of *Legum Sectio III* of *Monumenta Germaniae Historica*.
Guilhiermoz	P. Guilhiermoz, *Essai sur l'origine de la noblesse en France au moyen âge* (Paris, 1902).
HF	M. Bouquet and others, ed., *Recueil des historiens des Gaules et de la France*, 24 volumes (Paris, 1738–1904).
Mansi	J. D. Mansi and others, ed., *Sacrorum Conciliorum Nova et Amplissima Collectio*, 31 volumes (Florence and Venice, 1759–1798).
Migne, *PL*	J. P. Migne, ed., *Patrologiae Cursus Completus, Series Latina*, 221 volumes (Paris, 1862–1864).
MGH	*Monumenta Germaniae Historica*.
SS	*Scriptores* series of *Monumenta Germaniae Historica*.
Waitz	Georg Waitz, *Deutsche Verfassungsgeschichte*, I (3rd ed., Berlin, 1880); II (3rd ed., Berlin, 1882); III (2nd ed., Berlin, 1883); IV (2nd ed., Berlin, 1885).

INDEX

INDEX

Abbots, *see* Ecclesiastical functionaries
Abd-Allah, son of the late emir of Cordova, 62
Abd-er-Rahman, emir of Cordova, 62
Abraham, vidame of the bishop of Le Mans, and homage, 52
Actus Pontificum of Le Mans, cited, 52, 64
Adalgarius, archbishop of Hamburg, 53, 77
Adventius, bishop of Metz, 65
Agbertus, count, 47
Aldrici Episcopi Cenomannici Memoriale, text drawn from, concerning vassalage, 40, 41; probably a forgery, 41–42
Aldricus, bishop of Le Mans, commendation of, 63, 64, 77
Altmarus, seneschal of the queen, 41
Amici, 72
Annales Bertiniani, cited, 14, 27
Annales Einhardi, cited, 27, 28, 39, 90
Annales Fuldenses, cited, 23, 27
Annales Fuldenses Einhardi, cited, 39
Annales Laureshamenses, cited, 37, 38, 39; text drawn from, concerning vassalage, 35; second text concerning vassalage, 36, 40
Annales Mosellani, cited, 39
Annales Petaviani, cited, 39
Annales Regni Francorum, cited, 27, 28, 39, 90, 93

Annales Sithienses, cited, 39
Anscharius, archbishop of Hamburg, 65
Arnaldus, bishop of Tours, 58
Arno, archbishop of Salzburg, 64
Arnulf, king of the East Franks and emperor, and commendation of dukes of the Bohemians, 62

Bavaria, duchy of, 24–26; and Pepin, 27; and Charlemagne, 28–30. *See also* Tassilo III, duke of Bavaria
Bavo, vassal and fidelis of Louis the Pious, 59
Bernard, puppet king of Italy, one of the proceres of Louis the Pious, 61
Bishops, *see* Ecclesiastical functionaries
Bloch, Marc, views about oath of fidelity and commendation, 76; views about Carolingian vassalage, 81
Brazelavo, duke, 62
Broad and narrow interpretation of vassalage, *see* Interpretation of vassalage
Brunner, Henrich, views of Carolingian vassalage, 82; opinion regarding the bishops at Kiersy, *858*, 89

Calmette, J., views on oath of fidelity and commendation, 78
Capitulare Missorum Silvancense, cited, 65

INDEX

Capitularia De Disciplina Palatii Aquisgranensis, 14

Carloman, brother of Charlemagne, and Bavaria, 28

Carloman, Carolingian mayor, 25

Carloman, son of Louis II, 60, 77

Carolingian sources, and terminology of vassalage, 14

Charlemagne, establishes counts in Aquitaine, 15, 37; description of an encounter between Pepin and the Avars, 19; order of dining at the palace of, 21; and Bavaria, 28; prophetic words of, concerning Louis the German, 32; policy regarding grants, 34, 38; and pauperiores vassi sui, 35; division of the land of the Saxons, 36; and homage, 51–52; fideles under, 57, 59; and commendation, 62, 77; order of *805*, 78

Charles the Bald, commendation to, 14, 62; colloquium with Louis the German, 15; concessions in *856*, 17; use of cavalry under, 23; and fideles, 55; references to vassi and fideles, 59; diploma of, 59; and his nephew Pepin, 61; occupies Lorraine, 63, 77; and Wenilo, 64; meets Louis the German, *853*, 65; and the placitum at Pavia, *876*, 66; and the council of *876*, 67; commendation of bishops, counts, and vassals to, 75; invasion of his realm by Louis the German, 85–88

Charles the Fat, 15, 58, 62

Comites palatii as vassals, 47

Commendati, distinguished by function, 70; services of, 73. *See also* Commendation; Fideles

Commendation, 4, 5, 51, 80; and vassalage, 6, 7, 11, 48; of Tassilo III, duke of Bavaria, 26–28, 30; and fideles, 56, 57, 59; of royal servants, 61; and ecclesiastical functionaries, 66, 67; ranks among those commended, 71; historical continuity of, 72, 73; and vassalage, not identical, 73–74; and oath of fidelity, 75; essential to vassalage? 75, 83; relation to the oath of fidelity, 76–77; and private seigniors, 78

Continuity of development of vassalage, 73

Council of Attigny of *870*, 67

Council of Ponthion, *876*, 60

Counts, *see* Higher functionaries

Custodes, 72

Dahn, Felix, views of Carolingian vassalage, 80; opinion regarding the bishops at Kiersy, *858*, 89

Declareuil, J., views on the magnates and the vassi, 5

Dominus, definition of, 5. *See also* King, the

Dopsch, Alfons, views of Carolingian vassalage, 83

Drogo, bishop of Metz, 14

Dümmler, Ernst, opinion regarding Radbertus Paschasius, 45

Dumas, Auguste, interpretation of Tassilo text, 26; views about oath of fidelity and commendation, 75; views regarding Carolingian vassalage, 80

Ecclesiastical functionaries, and vassalage, 6, 7, 11, 12, 14, 15, 19, 21, 33, 35, 46, 49, 82, 83, 86, 89; duties of, 17, 19, 35; feudal status of, 62–63; as fideles, 63; and commendation, 63, 66, 67,

INDEX

68, 71; as missi, 65; and the king as seignior, 65, 68; and oath to their seigniors, 67, 68
Ehrenberg, Victor, views of Carolingian vassalage, 83, 84
Einhard, cited, 61
Eric, duke of Friuli, 61

Fideles, definition of and use of the term, 36, 38, 54, 58, 59, 68, 69; oath of, 56, 63; rewards to, 55; services due from, 55, 56; and commendation, 56, 57, 59; represent categories of royal subjects, 58; dukes included among, 58; applied to clergy and laity, 58; vassals as, 59; as royal servants in a more general sense, 60; and ecclesiastical functionaries, 64; relation to the king, 64; as commendati, 70; distinguished by functions, 70; term more appropriate than commendati, 73; conclusions concerning, 69-74; used to apply to men serving private seigniors, 78
Fighting forces, in Carolingian times, *see* Military forces, in Carolingian times
Flodoard, canon of Rheims, cited, 67-68
Fulco, comes palatii, 41, 42
Functionaries, ecclesiastical, *see* Ecclesiastical Functionaries
Functionaries, royal, *see* Higher functionaries; Lesser functionaries
Functions, of vassals, 18; of lower ranks of vassals, 48
Fustel de Coulanges, on the king, 5; interpretation of vassalage, 9; views on fideles, 97

Gasindi, 72
Gauziolenus, bishop of Le Mans, 52
Gerald, duke of Bavaria, 61
Gesta Aldrici, cited, 40, 64, 77
Gondreville, council of, *872*, 88
Grifo, half-brother of Pepin, 25
Guilhiermoz, P., 72; interpretation of vassalage, 8; views about oath of fidelity and commendation, 76
Guy of Spoleto, 66

Hadrian II, 61, 66
Handreichung, *see* Commendation
Harold, king of the Danes, commendation of, to Louis the Pious, 56, 62
Havet, J., and *Memoriale Aldrici*, 41
Hermintrude, wife of Charles the Bald, 65
Higher ecclesiastics, *see* Ecclesiastical functionaries
Higher functionaries, and vassalage, 6, 7, 12, 14, 15, 19, 31, 33, 35, 36, 46, 80, 82, 83; duties of, 16, 19, 34; differentiation between bishop, abbot, count, and vassal, 70
Hiltrude, mother of Tassilo III, 25
Hincmar, archbishop of Rheims, 16, 18; reference to oath of fideles, 58; as a fidelis, 67; his use of the word vassus, 72; and the synod of Kiersy, *858*, 85, 89
Hincmar, bishop of Laon, 18, 67
Hitto, bishop of Freising, 64
Homage, 6, 51, 75; case of Abraham, vidame of bishop of Le Mans, 52; ceremony of, 53; use

of the term, 53; liberi homines and, 54; secular nature of, 77
Homo, homines, 52, 68. *See also* Homage

Imbart de la Tour, Pierre, interpretation of vassalage, 10; views regarding the bishops at Kiersy, *858*, 89
Interpretation of vassalage, broad or narrow, 35–46

John, a fidelis of Charlemagne, 57
John VIII, 66

Kiersy, synod of, *858*, 85–89
King, the, in Carolingian times, his functions and resources, 4; his status, 5; relation of, to his subjects, 58; as rex, 64, 69; as seignior, 64, 69
Krawinkel, Hermann, interpretation of Tassilo's case, 90

Lesne, Émile, views of Carolingian vassalage, 83; and bishops at Kiersy, *858*, 89
Lesser functionaries, and vassalage, 16
Lex Alamanni, 16
Liberi homines, 54
Lot, Ferdinand, interpretation of Tassilo text, 26; views on Carolingian vassalage, 81
Lothair I, capitulary referring to homines, 54, 77
Louis the German, 15, 32, 33, 63, 65, 66; his invasion of the realm of Charles the Bald, 85–88
Louis the Pious, 14, 20, 32, 40, 41, 46, 51, 59, 63, 64, 82; inferior rank of vassals at the court of,

21; deposition of, 43; his sons as vassals, 43, 44; his use of the term vassal in a broader sense, 46; and Harold, king of the Danes, 56, 62; and fideles, 57
Louis II, 14, 16, 20, 60
Louis III, 60, 77
Lower ecclesiastical functionaries, and commendation, 64

Magnates, and vassalage, 6, 7, 31. *See also* Higher Functionaries
Memoriale Aldrici, see *Aldrici Episcopi Cenomannici Memoriale*
Military forces, in Carolingian times, 3
Military service, and vassalage, 18, 19–20, 22, 48; in Carolingian times, 4; transition from infantry to cavalry, 23
Milites, 72
Ministeriales as vassals, 15, 16, 47
Missi, and vassalage, 16; vassals used as, 17; ecclesiastical functionaries used as, 65; in *853*, 65
Mitteis, Heinrich, interpretation of vassalage, 9
Monk of St. Gall, description of ranks of vassals, 21; text concerning status of higher officials as vassals, 33–34; text drawn from, 32, 33; story about Louis the German, 46; story of Charlemagne's policy regarding lands given to counts and bishops, 46
Mühlbacher, E., and the *Memoriale Aldrici*, 41

Narrow interpretation of vassalage, 46. *See also* Interpretation of vassalage
Nomenoë, duke of Brittany, 62

INDEX

Oath of fidelity, and vassalage, 5, 6, 7; and ecclesiastics, 7; and Tassilo III, 26–28, 91; of the fideles, 56, 59, 63; of Kiersy, *858*, 58; to the seignior, 67, 78; and commendation, 75, 76–77; essential to vassalage? 75; religious nature of, 78; by whom sworn, 78–79
Odilo, duke of Bavaria, 25
Odo, bishop of Beauvais, 67
Optimates, *see* Proceres
Ordinary subject, in Carolingian times, 3

Palace counts, vassals as, 41
Pepin, Carolingian mayor, 25–28
Pepin, nephew of Charles the Bald, 61
Petot, Pierre, views about oath of fidelity and commendation, 76
Pfävers, monastery of, 43; Salomannus, abbot of, 47
Pfister, C., on commendation, 5; on vassi, 6
Pirenne, Henri, on vassalage as the basis of Carolingian government, 6
Placitum at Pavia, *876*, 66; *899*, 67
Poeta Saxo, cited, 39
Primores, use of term, 60, 63; superior to vassals, 60
Proceres, definitions of term, 60, 61. *See also* Higher functionaries
Pueri, 24, 72

Radbertus Paschasius, the *Vita Walae* of, cited, 43, 44; possible forgery, 46
Ragenarius, comes palatii, 41, 42
Respogius, son of duke of Brittany, 62

Rheims, council called at, *858*, 85
Rimbert, archbishop of Hamburg, 53
Robert, bishop of Le Mans, 41
Rodenberg, C., opinion of Radbertus Paschasius, 45
Roth, Paul, and the *Memoriale Aldrici*, 41
Royal functionaries, see Higher functionaries
Royal servants, as vassals, 5; terms used to describe, 5. *See also* Higher functionaries

St. Gall, monk of, *see* Monk of St. Gall
Salomannus, abbot of Pfävers, 47
Salomon, duke of Brittany, 62
Satellites, 24, 72
Seignior, definition of, 5; fideles commend themselves to a, 58; the king as, 64
Seigniors other than the king, as vassals, 11; and their dependents, 70
Servants, royal, ranks of, 21. *See also* Higher functionaries; Lesser functionaries
Senior, *see* Seignior
Services, as a means of supporting the state, in Carolingian times, 4; and vassalage, 11; and fideles, 56
Sicarii, 24
Sickel, Th., and the *Memoriale Aldrici*, 41
Simples vassaux, meaning of the term, 81
Simson, Bernhard, and the *Memoriale Aldrici*, 41; on Fulco and Regenarius, 42; his opinion of Radbertus Paschasius, 44, 45

INDEX

Subject, relation of to king, in Carolingian times, 3, 4, 58

Tassilo III, duke of Bavaria, case of 24–31, 33; broad and narrow interpretation of vassalage of, 47; Krawinkel's interpretation of case of, 90–96
Terminology of vassalage, 12, 14, 15
Theodo, son of Tassilo, 30
Tortoldus, bishop of Bayeux, 64

Vassalage, basis of Charlemagne's empire, 6; nature of, 6, 11; terminology of, 12; broad and narrow interpretation of, 35–46
Vassals, as royal servants, 5; and commendation, 5; various definitions of, 6, 7; "real," 11, 74; as used in Carolingian sources, 14; inferior rank of, 16, 21, 31, 33; in categories separate from ecclesiastics and higher functionaries, 16; duties of, 17, 18, 19, 20; and the seignior, 17; and military service, 20, 70; definition of, in Carolingian texts, 24; status of, under Charlemagne, 33, 35, 37; sons of the king as, 43, 44, 46; fighting functions of lower rank of, 48; various kinds of, 49; and the primores, 60; term not applicable to all royal servants in Carolingian times, 69; rarely synonymous with fideles, 71; loose use of term, 71; predecessors of, 72

Vassaticum, *see* Vassalage
Vassi dominici, 40, 81
Vassus, origin of word, 72
Viri fortes, 24, 72
Vita Hludowici Imperatoris, 14; text drawn from, and vassalage, 37, 38, 39; and use of the word vassus, 72
Vita Walae of Radbertus Paschasius, cited, 43
Vivianus, count and fidelis, 59

Waitz, Georg, interpretation of vassalage, 6–8, 76; on the identity of commendation and vassalage, 7; interpretation of text of the Monk of St. Gall, 32–34; and diploma of Louis II, 42; and homage, 53; views concerning the oath of fidelity and commendation, 76; and the bishops at Kiersy, *858*, 89
Walafrid Strabo, his comparison of secular and ecclesiastical government, 20
Welendus, Danish duke, and commendation, 62
Wenilo, bishop of Sens, 63, 64, 85
Werminghoff, A., and the *Memoriale Aldrici*, 41
Witzin, chief of a tribe of Slavs, 39–40, 47

Zatun, prefect of Barcelona, 62
Zwentibaldus, duke of the Moravians, 53, 62